Jazz Improvisation Fundamentals

Black & White Edition

by

Kenneth M. O'Gorman

Copyright Information

Jazz Improvisation Fundamentals,
Black and White Edition

Copyright © 2013 Kenneth M. O'Gorman
All Rights Reserved. Published 2013.

Visit our website at: www.OGormanMusic.com

any means, electronic, mechanical, photocopying, or otherwise without the prior written permission of the publisher.

The material in this book is furnished for informational use only and is subject to change without notice. The author and publisher assume no responsibility for any errors or inaccuracies that may appear in this book. The author and publisher assume no responsibility, warranty or liability for damages or losses of any kind in association with the contents within this book.

All material in this book was written by Kenneth M. O'Gorman (Ken O'Gorman). All images, logos, quotes and music in this book are subject to use according to copyright laws of the United States of America.

ISBN 13: 978-1494329396

10 9 8 7 6 5 4 3 2 First Publishing 2013

Word Cloud of the Topics in This Book

Jazz Improvisation Fundamentals

Table of Contents

About This Book 3
About This Method 4
What Is Jazz Improvisation? 5
Three Main Subjects 9
Terminology 11
Jazz Improvisation Fundamentals 33
Step-1 Decipher the Chord 35
   Root 40
   Chord Quality 42
      Major Triad 45
      Major Triad Extensions 47
   Dominant 7th Chord 48
      Undocumented Key Signatures 51
      Minor Triad 55
      Minor Extensions 56
      Augmented Triad 57
      Augmented Triad Extension 58
      Diminished Triad 59
      Diminished Triad Extensions 60
      Order of Chord Qualities 63
   Chord Extensions 67
   Chord Purpose 72
   Chord Tones Are Safe Tones 73

Jazz Improvisation Fundamentals

Step-1 Summary 74
Step-2 Associate a Scale 75
   Tones in a Chord Scale 81
   Chord Tones 82
   Passing Tones 83
      Scale Passing Tone 84
      Chromatic Passing Tone 85
   Step-2 Summary 86
Step-3 Play a Tone 87
   Here we go – Time to play! 90
   Improvise 93
   Change It Up 99
   Step-3 Summary 100
Improv Challenges 103
Exceptions to the Rule 109
   Other Scale Choices 113
   Minor Over Major 114
   Avoid the Root 116
   When the 3rd is NOT the 3rd 118
Substitutions 123
Staff Writing Exercise 129
Index 141
Other Training Materials 143

Introduction to Jazz Improvisation Concepts & Terminology

Jazz Improvisation Fundamentals

About This Book

This is my method of jazz improvisation. If other methods of jazz improvisation are failing you, give this one a try.

It's a very simple 3-step process that could fit onto a single page. However, there are explanations and exceptions that you may or may not be familiar with, so I expand on these topics as necessary.

This print version of the book includes music images so you have examples of what I am talking about*. To make things easy, most examples are in "C", but the concepts can be transposed to any key you desire.

This is not the only jazz improvisation method you should be aware of. To be well rounded, you should study as much varied material as you can. However, I believe this is an excellent approach for beginning improvisers, struggling intermediates looking to expand their ideas, and fellow jazz instructors who require a concise method for their students.

*eBook version does not contain music images.

About This Method

Nobody in the world enjoys helping you discover and improve your jazz improvisation skills more than me. It's quite rewarding, the way a student's eyes light up when they finally get it, when tone selections become enjoyable motifs, when they hit the stage and achieve a round of applause from a discerning audience.

I have done my best to take an otherwise difficult subject and put it into a logical 3-step process that could not be divided into any smaller element. That is, what you are about to learn is precisely what must occur in order for you to improvise; it's a fundamental approach. Leave out a step, and you will not succeed. Add to it, and you have easily surpassed minimum requirements to pull off a great solo. That's why I think this method is so significant – it just works!

What Is Jazz Improvisation?

This is a question that could easily have many answers depending on who you ask. If you ask me, Jazz Improvisation is basically "composing on the fly". That is, you ad-lib, or make-up something to play on the spot. In this book, you will learn to do so by performing select notes from scales that can be associated to the chords just above your music staff. I call it the Chord Tone/Passing Tone Method, or sometimes the 3-Step Approach.

Below, an image showing a C Chord Scale marked with Passing Tones.

You will use Chord Tones and Passing Tones to improvise later in this book.

Speaking of composing, did you know jazz has roots in classical music? Though the styles may be different, the way you improvise is the same way Bach, Brahms or Beethoven composed classical music. You may find that you use the same chord and scale associations in many places. Many of the melodic patterns jazz musicians employ come straight from classical music.

Classical musicians improvised hundreds of years ago. This is not an art solely for jazz musicians, and why I encourage musicians from every genre to try it. Many classical cadenzas were open areas for a virtuoso to perform as they wished, and later transcribed by others who wished to practice and perform that solo. Most seasoned musicians prefer to create or improvise their own solo in order to show off personal skill and creativity.

Jazz Improvisation is essentially composing on-the-fly.

Jazz Improvisation Fundamentals

Below is a clip from a classical score.

Notice the chords are shown above the music so you can see what the composer was thinking. Important items to notice:

1. Flute player gets a solo at the cadenza.

2. During first three beats of Dm, flute plays notes directly from a D Natural (Aeolian) Minor scale.

3. Beat four, flute enters upcoming A7 chord early, on purpose.

4. During the A7 chord, flute player substitutes the A Half-Whole Diminished (H-W Dim) scale with a few chromatic passing tones, rather than the usual choice, A Mixolydian. She does this because she personally finds the Mixolydian cliché and prefers the sound of the H-W Dim scale.

One thing that separates jazz from other forms of music, particularly small combo jazz, is that most music genres have a strongly defined melody, written out to be performed in a particular fashion, note for note. If there is a solo section, it is usually quite short in relationship to the rest of the song. Turn your radio to any classical, pop or rock channel and you will see what I mean.

Conversely, tune into a classic jazz channel playing small combo jazz, and you will likely hear a solo immediately, and have to wait a while before you hear the melody.

In combo jazz, the melody (or "Head" as jazz musicians refer to it) is relatively short and the solos quite long, comprising the majority of the song. Jazz musicians prefer this so they have a chance to show off individual skill and creativity, much like the classical virtuoso. In order to play an improvised solo, you must fully grasp the art and science of composing, particularly composing on the fly, or you will always struggle with your performance.

Does that mean we are going to have an in-depth discussion on composing? No! Fear not, we are not going to get that deep. This is not a PhD course; it's a guide for beginners and intermediates who still struggle with improvisation. In fact, I believe you will find this method quite easy to understand. Easy though it is, you truly are learning something about composing, and it will serve you all your days as a musician.

Three Main Subjects

Here are the main subjects in this book that will help you learn to improvise:

1. Decipher the Chord
2. Associate a Scale
3. Play Tones (Chord Tones or Passing Tones)

Those sound like big, scary, important subjects. They are actually a piece of cake. You will be improvising before you know it, with more confidence, direction and intention than ever before!

In the next section is terminology you should know before you begin reading the fundamentals.

Jazz Improvisation Fundamentals

Terminology

Here are a few terms and definitions you should understand before we continue:

Biad

A biad is a chord with only two notes. It's rare to see songs with biads in the chord progression. However, intervals such as Tritones performed in unison could be considered biads. When a bass player elects to play roots and 5ths rather than walk, that may be considered a biadic approach. When rock guitarists play "Power Chords", they actually play the root and 5th of a chord, which is essentially a biad.

Below, the Biads (in this case, Perfect 5ths) are the only notes used to express the chords.

Chart

In jazz, we call any song written on sheet music a "chart", as in, "Let's play the next chart then take a break." Or even, "Don't lose those charts; we have to return them later."

Jazz Improvisation Fundamentals

Chord

A chord is the simultaneous performance of several select notes, usually a triad, with one or more extensions and/or alterations.
Below, an example of a chord and chord symbol.

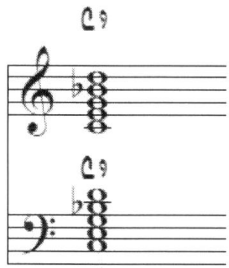

Chord Player

Chord players are those musicians who play polyphonic instruments capable of sounding several notes at one time. They are Piano, Guitar, Vibes, Marimba and occasionally Bass. These are the musicians providing you with chords you must address with appropriate scale associations to create your solo.

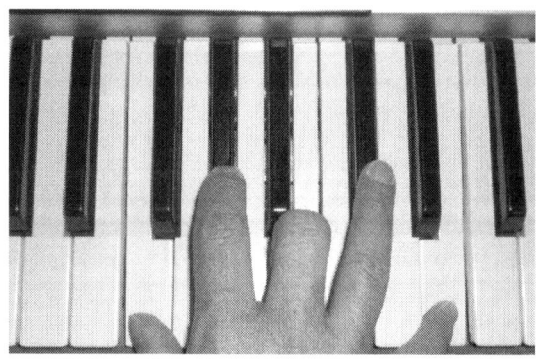

Jazz Improvisation Fundamentals

Chord Construction

Chords are normally derived from an associated scale. Chords usually have four notes, sometimes more, sometimes less. The four notes, or *Chord Tones,* are **properly called Root, 3rd, 5th, and 7th**, rather than First, Second, Third, and Fourth as the novice might have thought.

Chord construction may extend to 9th, 11th and 13th, which correlates to the notes found in the scale associated to the chord. Basic chord construction is usually performed against an intended scale association using the Keynote as a chord Root, followed by ascending intervals of thirds as derived from the associated scale.

Below, an example of the intervals (notes) making up a CMaj7 chord.

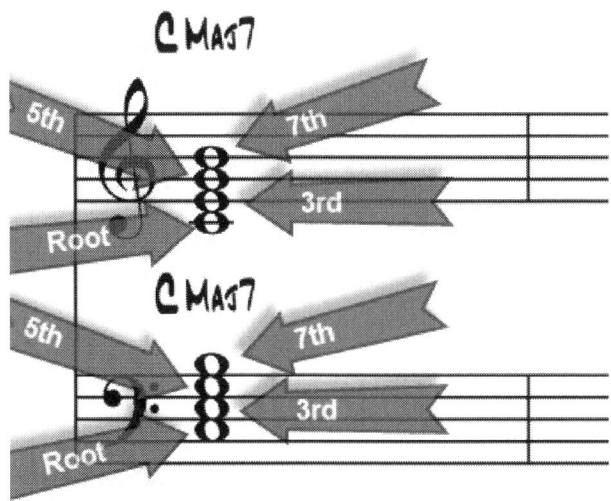

Chord Progression (Progression)

Just as the melody of a song progresses from verse to chorus, so does a series of chords which we call the *Chord Progression*, or simply "*Progression*". It's an integral part of the song form that provides the recognizable harmonic structure. It usually follows a particular arrangement along with the melody line and does not change. The Chord Progression usually repeats several times, once or twice with the melody ("Head"), as often as needed for the solo section, then one or two more times to restate the Head before the song ends.

Below, a song with a chord progression above the staff.

Song: "Bebop Blues", Copyright 2011 Kenneth M. O'Gorman.

Jazz Improvisation Fundamentals

Chord Scale

A scale that is associated to a chord. A palette of tones used to compose a song or improvise a solo. The association or combination of chord and scale equates to a Chord/Scale. Said in reciprocal, a Chord/Scale is the association of a chord and a scale.

Below, an example of a chord and scale association.

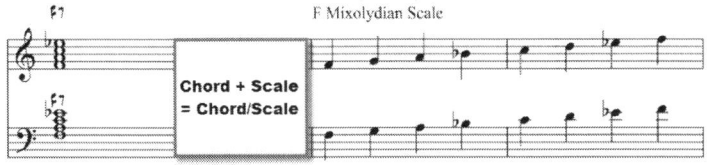

Chord + Scale = Chord/Scale

Chord Tones

The actual notes in a chord are the *Root, 3rd, 5th, and 7th, etc.* You may think that there are four notes in a chord and therefore they are numbered one, two, three, and four, but that is incorrect. There *are* four notes, but they are called Root, 3rd, 5th, and 7th.

These names come from numeric notation. Chords are associated to scales. Scales have degrees which are numbered. Chord names get their Identification or Root Name from this number. The Root of a chord matches the Keynote – the first note in a scale. The chord's 3rd is actually the 3rd note from the associated scale. The chord's 5th is the 5th note from the scale, etc.

There are exceptions where a few jazz scales have two 3rds in them. Those exceptions are discussed under "Exceptions" later in this book.

*Below, the four notes or "**Chord Tones**" of a C Major7 chord, i.e., The Root, 3rd, 5th and 7th.*

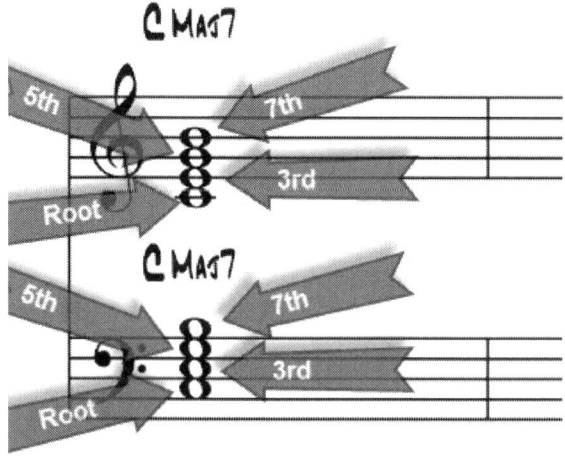

Chorus

The Chorus is often called the "B Section". A song may or may not have a chorus, but if there is one it will be the part of a song that usually follows the verse. The verse is often called the "Head" or "A Section" in jazz... more on that later. If there are lyrics to the chorus, they likely will not change each time through (unlike the verse which usually changes every time through).

The Chorus ("B Section") simply provides a new musical idea to make a song more interesting. Songs with a chorus often use the AABA song format.

Enharmonic

One note with two (or more) different names. Enharmonics sound exactly the same, and have the same fingering on your instrument when played. Example: **G#** and **Ab**. Another example is **A** and **Bbb** (that's B-double-flat, also called B Diminished).

Below, several enharmonic notes are depicted.

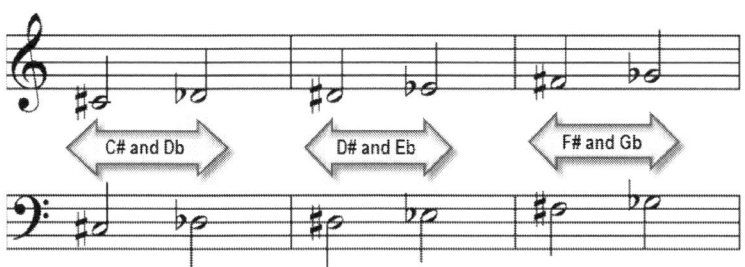

Extensions

    Notes added to a chord for a more interesting or unique harmonic quality.

Head

    Jazz musicians often call the melody the "Head" because it's at the top, and the main idea of the song.

Below, the "Head" or melody begins as indicated by the arrow, not counting the pickup.

Song: *"Bebop Blues", Copyright 2011 Kenneth M. O'Gorman.*

Intro

    Intro, or introduction, is often the first thing a musician plays to either help or support the upcoming melody.

Jazz Theory

Any music theory jazz musicians employ to achieve a musical goal or idea. Jazz theory is usually much more permissive than classic music theory, allowing for a wider range of acceptable music theory rules and concepts.

Last Four (Last 4)

Any time a musician calls out "Last Four", this means they want you to play the last four measures of the song.

If they hold out a hand with three fingers extended, they want you to repeat the last four measures of the song three times.

This is a very popular jazz outro, a way to "get out" of the song, i.e., end the song. It can also be used as "a way in", or Intro.

Example: "Last Four, then Head", means play the last four bars of the song and start at the very top.

Melody

The main musical statement of a song. The melody is often called the "Head" in jazz. It's the main idea of a song. Refer back to Head for an example image.

Jazz Improvisation Fundamentals

Monophonic Instrument

A musical instrument capable of sounding only one true note at a time. That includes most reed or brass instruments such as: clarinets, flutes, saxophones, trumpets, trombones, etc.

Below, a musician playing saxophone – a monophonic instrument.

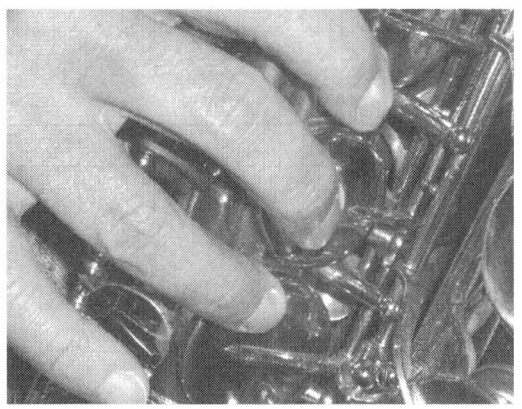

Numeric Notation

Each tone in a scale is numbered in order as a scale is played ascending (up). I call this numbering *Numeric Notation*. It is also referred to as Numbered Music Notation. The Keynote is numbered one, and is always the first note in a scale, giving it its namesake. The Keynote always corresponds to its associated chord's ROOT. In fact the Keynote is often incorrectly called the Root, which is okay on the street but perhaps not a college classroom.

Below, Numeric Notation Example – The C Major Scale spelled out with Numeric Notation below each note.

C-1, D-2, E-3, F-4, G-5, A-6, B-7, C-8

Outro

Also called an exit or ending, the outro is just a means to break away from the melody to end the song.

In classical music, you might call this a "D.C." or "D.S. al Coda/Fine", etc. If a song ends with the melody, like *"My Funny Valentine" by Richard Rodgers and Lorenz Hart*, there may be no outro, just a ritardando and that's it – you are out. Some songs play through the melody, then end or "go out" with a different idea, or outro. *"A Night in Tunisia" by Dizzy Gillespie* is the perfect example of a song with both an intro and an outro.

Passing Chord

A passing chord is usually every other chord in a chord progression that is not the all-important Tonic Chord. Passing chords add an interesting tonal change that makes the music more enjoyable to the listener, and more challenging to an improviser.

If you consider a song with only one chord in it, (likely the Tonic) from start to finish, you may have just considered the world's most boring song.

Add a few chords that pass from the Tonic to a few other chords before coming back to the Tonic and suddenly the song becomes much more interesting.

Passing Tone

In traditional classic music theory, a Passing Tone (PT) is actually a neighboring tone that ascends. In Jazz Theory, a passing tone is simply any non-chord tone.

You use passing tones to literally *pass* from one chord tone to another, usually giving your solo a balance of harmony and dissonance. You can hold out a Passing Tone for a little while, emphasizing the dissonance, especially if you follow it up with a Chord Tone for a pleasant resolution.

Jazz Improvisation Fundamentals

Below, Chord Tones and Passing Tones are shown on the Grand Staff, represented by **Chord** *or* **Pass**:

Polyphonic Instrument

A musical instrument capable of performing several notes at one time, such as: piano, guitar, mallets, bass, etc. Polyphonic instrumentalists may be referred to as "Chord Players" because they are capable of playing whole chords.

Below, a jazz musician holding his guitar, a polyphonic instrument.

Jazz Improvisation Fundamentals

Rhythm Section

The standard jazz rhythm section consists of Drums, Bass, Piano, and Guitar. The rhythm section lays down the rhythms and chords for a soloist to play over or against.

Slashed Notation

Jazz musicians crave measures of slashed notation. It indicates that this is a measure in which you should improvise. Slashed notation is a form of music notation that takes the place of actual notes on your music staff. There is usually a chord above it, if not then you are to use the chord from the previous measure. The slash symbol leans from left to right. The number of slashes in a measure matches the beats per measure, usually 3 or 4 slashes.

Below, a section of music containing slashed notation.

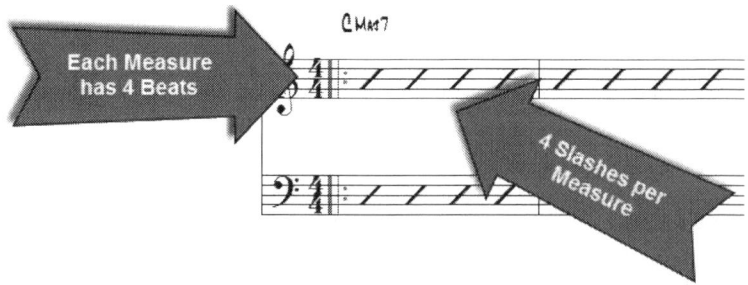

Jazz Improvisation Fundamentals

Song Form AABA

There are many song forms, but AABA is one of the most used in any genre. AABA implies that the verse, main melody, or "Head" should be played, then repeated; hence "AA". After that the chorus should be played (the "B Section"), followed by the verse one more time (A). This all makes up the complete AABA song form. Any improvised solos will then follow that same form, AABA, or occasionally just solo over the A section. There are many other song forms, in fact too many to list, but no matter what the song form entails, usually the solos will follow that form, with only a few exceptions. A few other song forms you will encounter are: AA, AABC, ABABC, etc.

Below a song with an A Section and a B Section.

Song: "The Parrot", Copyright 2012 Kenneth M. O'Gorman.

Substitutions

Chords or scales that you select for use instead of the chords or scales suggested in your music. "Subs" are usually related harmonically in some way to the chords/scales you are replacing or "subbing".

If you are a beginner, you should not perform substitutions until you can improvise using the chords already suggested by your music. This will be explained in greater detail under "Advanced Tips" near the end of the book.

Below, an example of a substitute, playing a G Dorian scale over a C7 chord.

Trade-Fours

Musicians often like to have fun soloing with each other by performing something called "Trading-Fours". A musician desiring to trade-fours with a fellow musician will often cue that person by holding up 4 fingers of a free hand. The musician initiating the trading will simply play a short motif (also called a lick, riff, run, or pattern – whatever you wish to call it) that lasts four bars. The solo is then passed to the second musician, who will then play a riff lasting four bars. The first musician will then play another riff, with the second musician answering back with a four bar riff, and so the cycle repeats as long as desired.

Though we call this, "trading-fours", it's not required to keep the motifs at four bar lengths. You could perform eight-bar lengths, or even two bar lengths. You can even trade very short riffs back and forth that are less than a complete measure; however, it often begins with musicians signaling a desire to trade-fours.

Tritone

A Tritone describes the interval of either an augmented 4th, or a diminished 5th. In either case, the same pitches are achieved, creating both an interval and a sound called a tritone. Tritones can exist inside of chords, in particular the diminished chord and its many variants. Tritones may be performed simultaneously as a two-note chord (Biad), or as arpeggios.

Below, an example of Tritones.

Tonic Chord

Below, a song with the Key signature and matching Tonic chord clearly marked with arrows.

It's very important for musicians to identify and understand the Tonic Chord, or simply "The Tonic". You may also hear it called "The One" or "The One Chord". It is a very important chord, and matches the key signature, providing the main tonal quality of a song. In many cases, you will improvise your solo and come home to the Tonic. Even if a song takes you through many key changes that are unmarked, you will always come home to, or "Play for" the Tonic.

For example, if a Song is in E Minor, the Tonic chord is Em (E-) or a form of that chord (E-7, Em9, E-9) and the appropriate scale to associate with it is one of the many possible E Minor scales. If a song is in C Major, then the Tonic chord is a form of C Major, i.e., C, C6, CMaj7, CMaj9, etc.

In jazz, the tonal quality and key signature often changes throughout the song, but usually returns to the original key sometime before ending. Most songs start and stop on the Tonic Chord, or a progression that leads to it. Most turn-arounds and other ii-V-I (2-5-1) progressions resolve to the Tonic.

For example, the jazz ballad *"Misty" by Erroll Garner* is in Concert EbMajor. The song starts on EbMaj7 and ends on EbMaj7. Read the music sometime and notice the EbMaj7 (Eb in its simpler triadic form) matches the key signature, Eb Concert. The Key and Chord have the same Keynote/Root, which makes Eb Maj7 the Tonic Chord. Every other chord is just a passing chord, a trip you must take on your musical journey, before returning home to the Tonic.

Below, an image depicting the last chord of the song is usually the Tonic Chord, which matches the Key Signature.

Jazz Improvisation Fundamentals

Triad

A chord made of only three notes. Most chords are built upon a basic triad. Any chord listed with no extensions is specifying the basic triad.

Example 1: C by itself is a C triad, played on your instrument is: C, E, G.

Example 2: Eb by itself is an Eb triad, played on your instrument is: Eb, G, Bb.

Triads have four primary qualities. They are:

- Major
- Minor
- Augmented
- Diminished

There is much more information on these basic triads and their likely extensions later in this book.

Below are samples of triads you will encounter.

Major Triad

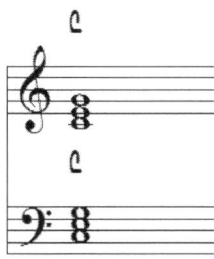

Jazz Improvisation Fundamentals

Minor Triad

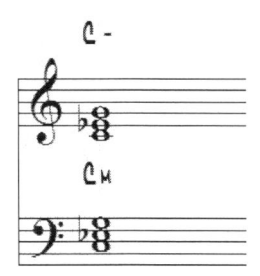

Augmented Triad

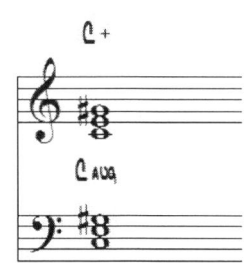

Diminished Triad

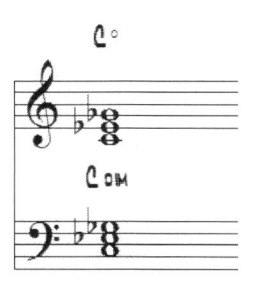

Turn-Around

    A turn-around is a short chord progression that resolves to the Tonic Chord, and is easily repeatable and extendable. A turn-around is usually a ii-V-I (2-5-1) progression or one of its many variations.

Turn-arounds are quite prevalent in music, especially in jazz. They can comprise an entire song, or be used as an intro/outro to a song. Turn-arounds can support a written melody, a phrase ending, or establish a place to solo. They are a popular place for the band leader to talk to the audience, usually to introduce the band. Turn-arounds are also a great place for a musician to take extended solos or Trade-Fours with other musicians.

Below, a 2-5-1 (I-VI-II-V) turn around that could be repeated for eternity.

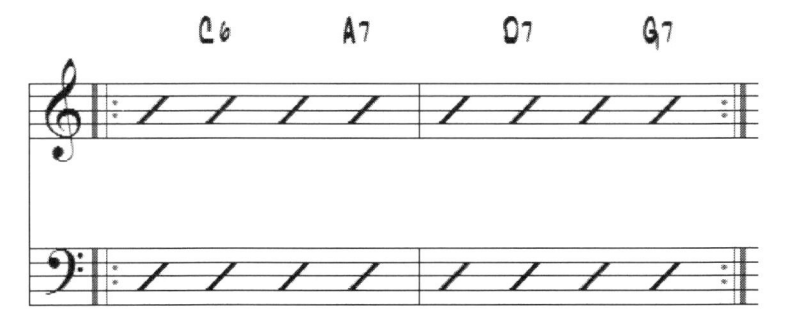

C6   A7   D7   G7

Verse

The verse of a song is usually the main idea, or melody, and may be played once, or have repeats. It's often referred to in jazz as the "Head" or "A" section, and is identified on the sheet music with a capital letter "A". The verse may include lyrics that change each time through, or it may be an instrumental melody with no lyrics. The verse may or may not lead to a Chorus or "B Section", depending on the composer's wishes.

Jazz Improvisation Fundamentals

Jazz improvisation (improv) may seem overwhelming at first. However when you break it down into its lowest common denominator, you find three basic tasks you must perform, which I call "improv fundamentals".

You must perform all three improv fundamentals otherwise you won't be able to improvise successfully. I have arranged the three fundamentals into three logical steps to make jazz improvisation easier and attainable.

This method is not limited to the novice. You could easily apply these three steps into a highly complicated outside solo with all kinds of extensions or substitutions.

Remember earlier, when I said I could fit my method on a single page? Here you go… in fact it is not even an entire paragraph:

3-Step Jazz Improvisation Method

1. Decipher the Chord
2. Associate a Scale
3. Play the Tones

That's it. Repeat that process until the solo is over. Anything else is simply supporting material for the fundamental 3-steps. You can and should do this on any and every chord you encounter in your music.

Now, those three steps each have a copious amount of supporting material which could easily turn into a college course. However, any extension, alteration, substitution, etc., can be classified as a sub-step of the main three steps.

This method works no matter what style jazz you play: Bebop, Big Band, Classic, Contemporary, Dixieland, Funk, Fusion, Smooth, etc.

As I said, you could spend years, decades, even a lifetime studying the depth and complexity of each step, so let's get started.

Step 1

Decipher The Chord

Step-1 Decipher the Chord

If you know how to decipher a chord and all its implied chord tones, move on to step two. If not, please read on.

You absolutely must be able to identify chords and decipher all the notes (or tones) in the chord, because you will use them all the time. In fact, chord tones are the single most appropriate notes you can play in any solo.

Furthermore, chords associate with scales, and vice-versa. You must be able to determine all the notes in a chord in order to successfully associate a scale. Let's take a closer look at this.

Above every measure (or "bar") is a ***Chord Symbol,*** which implies specific ***Chord Tones***. It's the letter with several possible symbols following it. The average chord is a simple triad with one or more extensions.

You absolutely <u>must</u> be able to identify chords and decipher all the notes (tones) in the chord.

Below, Chord Symbols are circled for easy identification.

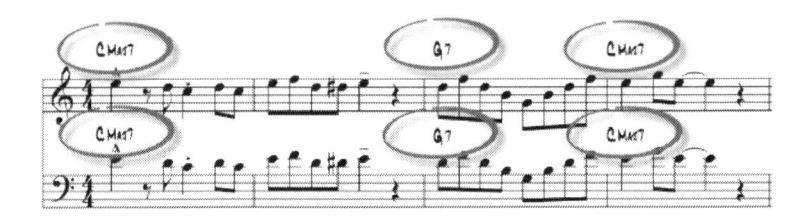

Notice in the above example, there is no chord in measure two. This indicates you are to continue using the chord from the previous measure (in this case, CMaj7) until a new chord change is encountered.

    Chords are built from degrees of an associated scale. An associated scale is simply a scale that you find appropriate to play over a chord, and usually has matching Root/Keynote, 3rds, 5ths, 7ths, etc. Each note in the scale is a degree that matches the notes in a chord.

Here is an example of a chord: C-7, which could also be written as Cm7. Spoken aloud, you would call this a "C Minor Seven". This C-7 (or Cm7) consists of the *Chord Root*, the *Chord Quality*, and *Chord Extensions*. Let's break this down.

Below is a C-7 chord. C-7 = (C, Eb, G, Bb) also sometimes written as Cm7.

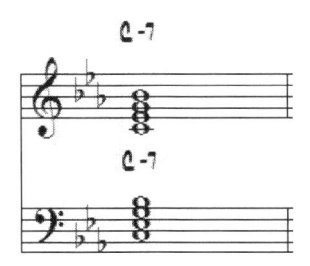

- The C is the **Root**, the tonal foundation the chord is built upon.

- The minus sign "-" (or "m") indicates **minor quality,** therefore a basic minor triad (C,Eb,G).

- The "7" indicates **minor 7th** on top, in this case "Bb".

Root

Chords always start with a letter that corresponds to an actual note the chord is built upon, in this case "C". This note is also called the "Chord Root", or just "Root". It is the tonal foundation of the chord. Every other note in the chord is just harmonic support to make it sound full and interesting.

If a chord were **F#7**, the root would be **F#**. If the chord were **Adim7**, the root would be **A**.

Below, notice the Chord Symbol's letter name always matches the chord's Root, in this case, F#.

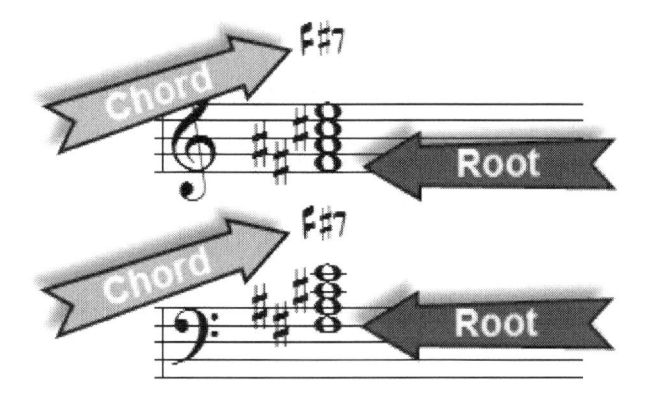

*Below, another example showing the Chord Symbol's letter name will always match the root, in this case, A^o7, also called **Adim7**.*

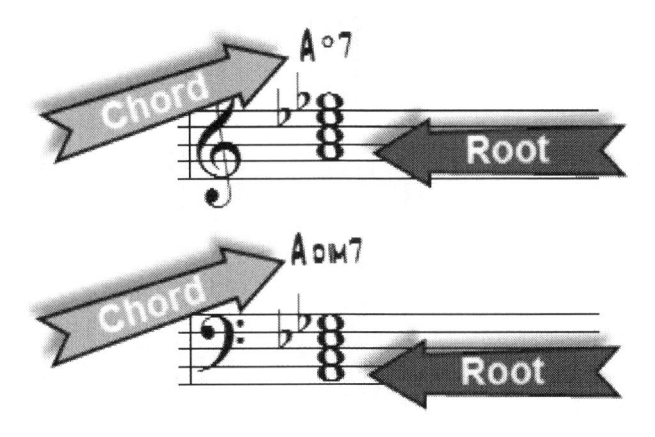

The chord's root always matches the chord symbol's letter.

Jazz Improvisation Fundamentals

Chord Quality

You determine a chord's quality by the various letters and numbers, or lack thereof, that come after the Chord letter. If you remember from the previous section, the Chord's letter name tells us the Root note for the chord.

The chord quality refers to the basic triad that the rest of the chord is built upon. The 3rd and 5th of a triad is what determines the triad's quality. This is important to understand because most chords are built upon one of the four primary triads.

The four primary triad qualities that most chords are built upon are: Major, Minor, Augmented, and Diminished.

Primary Triad Qualities:
Major
Minor
Augmented
Diminished

Extensions can change the nature of a chord but for now, let's only discuss the triad.

Chord quality changes the overall sound of the chord, and even specifies which scale you should associate to the chord. For example:

- Major chords usually associate with Major scales.

- Minor chords usually associate with Minor scales.

- Augmented chords usually associate with Augmented (Whole-Tone) scales.

- Diminished chords usually associate with Diminished scales.

Remember, I said *usually*. In later studies you will learn to substitute minor scales over major chords, but not until you understand basic chord-scale associations. "You gotta walk before you can run." That may not be the most grammatically correct sentence, but the sentiment is spot on.

Chord qualities are discussed further in the following sub-sections.

Major chords usually associate with Major scales.

Minor chords usually associate with Minor scales.

Augmented chords usually associate with Augmented (Whole-Tone) scales.

Diminished chords usually associate with Diminished scales.

Chord Quality:

- **Changes the overall sound of the chord**
- **Specifies which scale you should associate to the chord**

Jazz Improvisation Fundamentals

Major Triad

Numeric Notation: 1, 3, 5
Example: C = C, E, G

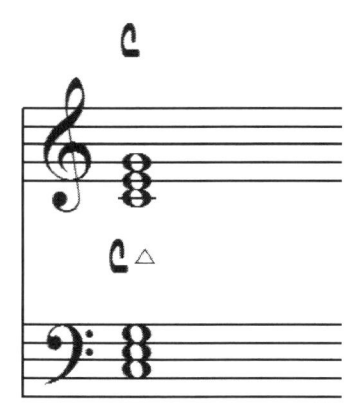

Note: a small **triangle** next to a chord symbol implies the basic triad is **major**.

If there is no letter to indicate chord quality after the chord letter, (as in C7 or F6) then the base triad is Major. To reiterate, no quality implies Major, that is, a major triad is the foundation of the chord.

A Major triad has a Major 3rd in it, which gives it its name, so long as the 5th is still Perfect (unaltered by lowering or raising with accidentals).

Major Triad Extensions

- Adding a Major 6th to a Major triad creates a Major 6th Chord.

- Adding a Major 7th to a Major triad creates a Major 7th Chord.

- Adding a 9th to a Major 7th chord creates a Major 9th Chord.

This leads to another section called "Dominant 7th Chord", a subset of Major.

- Adding a minor 7th to a Major triad creates a Dominant 7th Chord.

- Adding a Minor 9th to a Dominant 7th chord creates a Dominant 7th/Flat 9th chord.

- Adding a Major 9th to a Dominant 7th chord creates a Dominant 9th Chord.

Jazz Improvisation Fundamentals

Dominant 7th Chord

Dominant 7th chords are similar to other major chords. They are built upon a major triad which is why I list them as a subset of Major. Other instructors prefer to create a separate class for Dom7, but I don't think that's necessary as long as you properly associate the correct scale to the chord.

Below, an example of adding a minor 7th to a major triad to create a Dominant 7th chord.

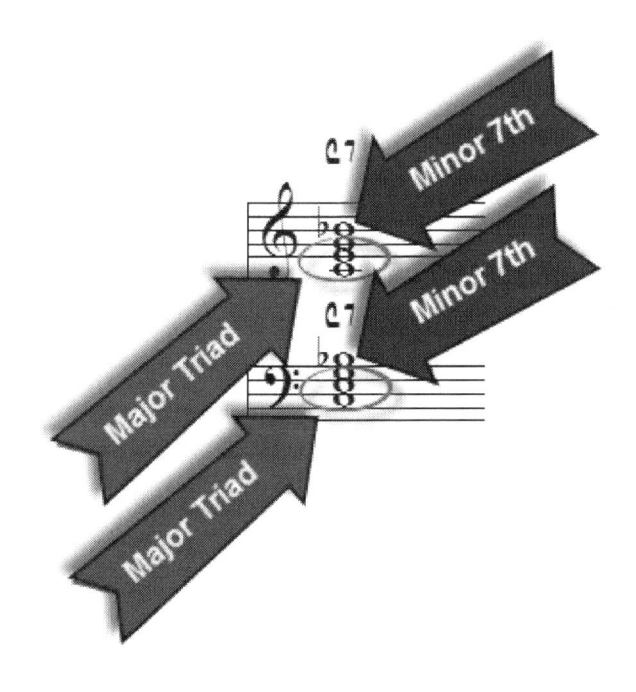

You address this chord like any other, by playing tones from its associated scale.

Here is where some confusion comes into play. If you have studied classical music theory, then you have studied modes. You know that the 5th mode of Major is Mixolydian, which associates to a Dominant chord. Furthermore, your Dominant chord usually resolves to Tonic, and cannot stand on its own as a Tonic chord.

Now stop right there and put that moldy concept away – this is jazz!

In most forms of music *besides* classical, a Dominant 7th chord can be the tonic! You have likely been playing from fake books and have seen it plain-as-day, but not given it much thought. If you will go back and look at your fake books, you will find that more songs than not use a Dom7 as Tonic – the tonal foundation of the song or current chord progression.

Jazz Improvisation Fundamentals

Below, an image showing a Dominant 7th chord is the Tonic chord in a song keyed as Bb Major. The Root of the Tonic Chord always matches the Key signature. However, beware the key signature may be undocumented!

Song: "Bebop Blues", Copyright 2011 Kenneth M. O'Gorman.

Undocumented Key Signatures

Undocumented key signatures are a somewhat advanced concept, but you should understand them in light of the previous example where the tonic chord's root always matches the key signature.

In jazz, undocumented key changes occur frequently, often only for a few measures. It is not appropriate to change the entire song's key signature for only a few measures, something advanced improvisers understand.

A perfect example is the classic, *"Have You Met Miss Jones?" by Richard Rodgers and Lorenz Hart*, in F Major (concert key). The song starts out in F Major and progresses nicely through several 2-5-1s. Then comes the bridge, which stymies the new improviser.

During the bridge, there are several 2-5-1s (ii-V-I) that move by descending Major 3rds. Each "ii-V" leads to its home chord, the "I" (a Tonic), which only persists for a short time. It's too short a progression to change the key of the entire song but the Tonic truly implies a new key, albeit short-lived, substantiated by the ii-V leading to it.

The improviser must respond to each of the Tonics in turn, which eventually ii-V-I back to the original key. It's important to note, if you try to play the bridge in the original key (F Major), you sound dissonant and lost because you are not addressing the chords presented to you. There is no single "magic scale" to cover every scenario. Learn to find the Tonics and how to play them, and you will be well on the road to expertise and understanding.

Always remember that a 2-5-1 is a journey that eventually leads you to some kind of "1" (One, I, or Tonic), however you wish to view it. There are many more chord progressions than this, but once you understand the function of a 2-5-1, you will be able to correlate what you know into any other progression.

This is much more advanced than I wish to include in a fundamentals book, but I wanted to give you a glimpse of where the fundamentals are leading you.

I have always believed if that you can't improvise over a single chord with a single scale, you will be utterly lost playing advanced chord progressions leading to a Tonic that is moving out of the song's original key, as I just demonstrated with *"Have You Met Miss Jones?"* After reading and practicing the fundamentals I am teaching you, all this will eventually make much more sense. Let me say this once again: learn to walk before you run.

Back to that Dominant 7th chord...

Technically, when you use modal scales without regard to relative function, you are using Parallel Modes. In other words, you wind up using a scale that is "shaped" like a mode, but applying it directly to a chord, with no intention to satisfy its purpose in classical theory. For example, the C Mixolydian scale pairs up nicely with a C7 chord.

That being said, you do not have to conform to the rules classical theorists apply to the Dominant 7th chord. Treat it like any other chord, not as a chord with some special meaning or function that must lead to some other chord. You simply play it like any other chord, and the Root is the tonal foundation for as long as it is the current chord.

To play over a Dom7 chord, you will use a Mixolydian scale. Notice I said scale, not mode. Saying "Mode" implies you are using the 5th degree of a related but different scale. We are not doing that. We are using directly associated scales with our chords. The Root and Keynote should match.

You can read more about relative and parallel modes in my book, <u>Scales A La Mode</u>. It has a ton of explanations about this, plus exercises, examples, and even a link to free online play-alongs you can use to practice.

Below, a C Dominant 7 chord with associated C Mixolydian scale. Notice Chord Root and Scale Keynote match.

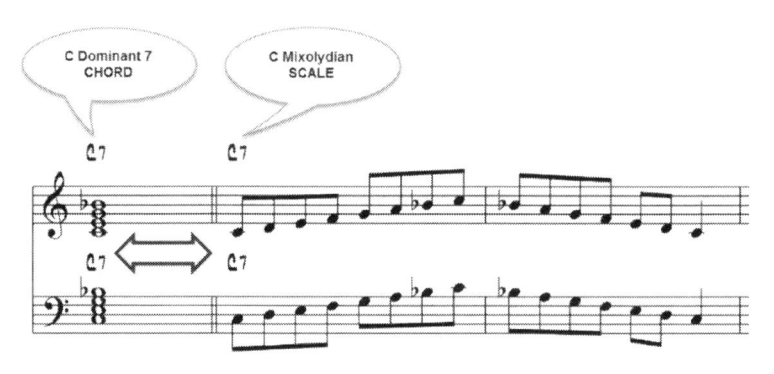

For example, if a song is in C Major, and the Tonic chord is a C7 (which could not happen in classical music but does in every other genre), then the Tonic chord is C7. What scale should you use to play over C7? The answer is: C Mixolydian scale. Not F Major as the classical cross-over often assumes, but C Mixolydian. You may also call it a *C Dominant 7 Scale*, or "C Mix", short for Mixolydian.

We haven't really gotten into scales yet, which is the next chapter. But remember going forward that the scale's keynote should match the chord's root (until you get into advanced improvisation, where you experiment with substitutes).

Minor Triad

Example: Cm = C, Eb, G
Numeric Notation = 1, b3, 5

Below, a C minor chord (Cm or C-) depicted on the Grand Staff.

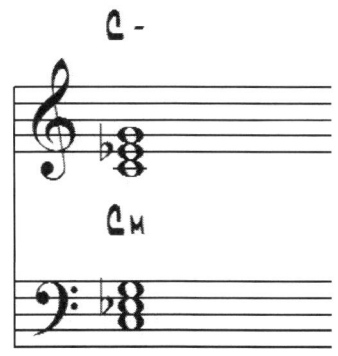

       Lower case "m" or a minus sign "-" indicates that a minor triad is the foundation of the chord. Whenever a Major 3rd is lowered a half-step, it becomes a minor 3rd. This minor third is what gives the chord its quality, provided the 5th is still Perfect (not lowered or raised by accidentals).

       Fonts in modern music software often use a smaller form of the capital letter, such as "$_M$". This makes it difficult to identify a chord as minor or major. Remember this, if there is a lone "$_M$" by itself with no other letters such as "Ma" "Maj" or "Major" then the chord in question should be assumed *minor*.

Minor Extensions

- Adding a Major 6th to a Minor triad creates a minor/Major 6th Chord.

- Adding a Minor 7th creates a Minor 7th Chord.

- Adding a Major 7th creates a Minor/Major 7th Chord.

Below an example of the CmMaj7 Chord.

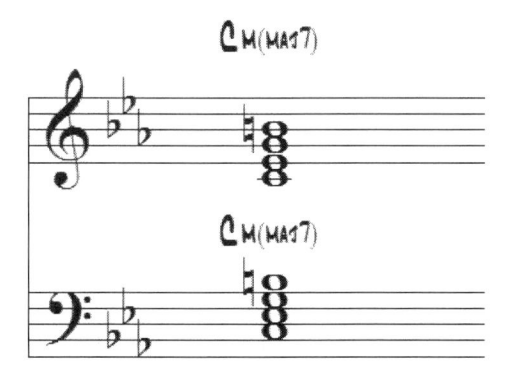

A lone "ₘ" usually implies MINOR, even if the letter appears to be a capital.

Augmented Triad

Example: CAUG (also C+) = C, E, G#
Numeric Notation: 1, 3, #5

Augmented chords have a Root, a Major 3rd and an Augmented 5th. Augmented is indicated by a plus sign, "+" or "AUG".

Here are a few examples of Augmented chords:
- C+ = (C, E, G#)
- Db AUG = (Db, F, A)
- E+7 = (E, G#, B#, D)
- G AUG 7 = (G, B, D#, F)

Jazz Improvisation Fundamentals

Augmented Triad Extension

The most common extension you will find above augmented triads is the minor 7th.

- Adding a Minor 7th creates an Augmented 7th Chord.

Below, an image depicting the C+7, or CAug7 chord.

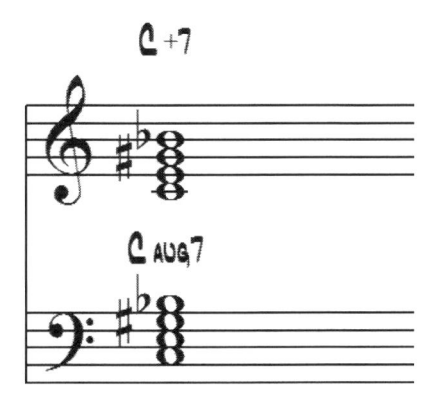

Trivia Question:

Name a chord where it's okay to have both a Flat *and* a Sharp in it?

Answer:

The C Augmented 7th chord. It has a G# and a Bb, and it's all legal! The Augmented 5th makes the G#. The Minor 7th makes the Bb.

Diminished Triad

Numeric Notation: 1, b3, b5
Example: C Dim = C, Eb, Gb

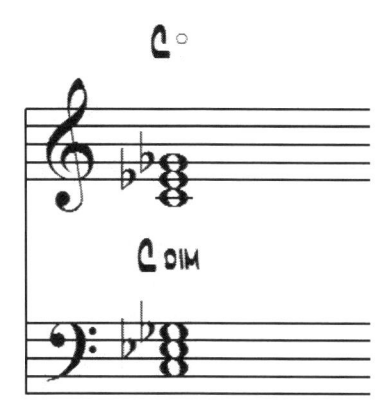

Diminished triads have a Root, minor 3rd and a diminished 5th. Whenever you lower a 5th in a scale it's called a diminished 5th, not a minor 5th. This diminished 5th is what gives a diminished chord its quality.

Depending on the type of 7th you add to a diminished chord, you achieve two different chords that require two different kinds of diminished scale. They are Diminished 7th, and Half-Diminished which is usually called the Minor 7th/Flat-Five chord. Let's expand on this.

Diminished Triad Extensions

Adding a 7th to the diminished triad, you achieve two kinds of diminished chord. They are *Diminished 7th (or fully diminished)* and *Half-Diminished (or Minor Seventh Flat Five)*. Both have a basic diminished triad (1, b3, b5), but it's the 7th that determines which is full diminished, or half-diminished. Let's look at each more closely.

Diminished Symbol °

A small un-broken circle (o) implies a diminished triad, but does not necessarily include a 7th on top. However, if a 7th is indicated, it will be a diminished 7th, not a minor 7th.

Half-Diminished Symbol ø

A small circle with a slash (ø) implies half-diminished. A diminished triad includes a minor 7th on top, even if the 7th is not indicated in the chord. This is commonly called a Minor-7th Flat-5th, or m7(b5).

Let's examine these more closely.

Diminished 7th Chord

Numeric Notation: 1, b3, b5, bb7

Example 1:
Cdim7 = C, Eb, Gb, Bbb (or C, Eb, Gb, A)

Example 2:
C°7 = C, Eb, Gb, Bbb (or C, Eb, Gb, A)

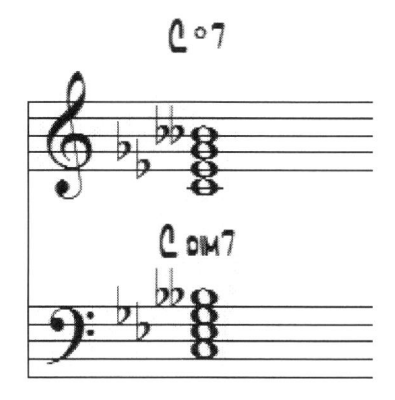

Diminished 7th chords start out with a diminished triad but also have a diminished 7th, i.e., a double-flat 7th. A diminished 7th is achieved when you take a minor 7th and lower it one more chromatic half-step. That makes the chord formulae in numeric notation look like this: 1, b3, b5, bb7.

However, for sake of ease, many musicians will describe the "Dim7" chord as 1, b3, b5, 6. That's because the 6 (Major 6th) is enharmonic to a diminished 7th. In C that is: C, Eb, Gb, Bbb (or C, Eb, Gb, A).

Half-Diminished (Minor-7th, Flat-5) Chord

Numeric Notation: 1, b3, b5, b7

Example 1:
Cm7(b5) = C, Eb, Gb, Bb

Example 2:
Cø or Cø7 = C, Eb, Gb, Bb

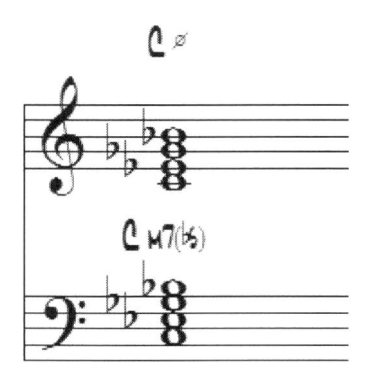

    Half-Diminished chords are often called a "Minor Seventh Flat-Five", or m7b5. An example is Cm7(b5). This chord has a diminished triad with a minor 7th on top. This is the chord where you finally get to use that Locrian mode scale or even the half-whole diminished scale. The full chord is 1, b3, b5, b7. In C that is: C, Eb, Gb, Bb.

Order of Chord Qualities

The order of chord (or triad) qualities is:

1. Major
2. Minor
3. Augmented
4. Diminished

Major

     Major usually comes first in a list of triads or chord qualities. This is because major has no accidentals in contrast to the key signature, and is considered the easiest key to play.

Minor

     Minor is considered second in a list of triads or chord qualities. Minor is related to major, but is often viewed as more difficult to play because most students learn major first. In fact, natural (Aeolian) minor keys are related (sharing the same key signature as a relative major key) and actually no harder to play than major keys, yet are often perceived as more difficult to perform and understand. Also, minor chords are encountered much more frequently than augmented chords. Finally, major and minor keys actually exist and can be notated on staff paper, while augmented and diminished keys do not exist. This is why minor comes second in a list of quality.

Augmented

Because there is no key signature to support augmented keys, and because augmented chords can only exist with accidentals (the raised 5th or augmented 5th), augmented is third in a list of chord qualities.

The only way to achieve an augmented triad or chord is with an accidental (a raised 5th, hence Augmented 5th). While there is an associated augmented scale, called the Whole Tone scale, there is no key signature to cover augmented chords, and therefore they do not exist as naturally like Major and Minor.

Diminished

Diminished chords are last in the order of chord quality because, like augmented, they do not have their own key signature. Furthermore, they have the most altered tones of any other chord type. The 3rd is minor, and the 5th is diminished, giving the chord its quality.

Like augmented chords, diminished chords have several associated diminished scales, but do not have an associated key signature, due to all the lowered tones in the chord.

Suspended

Suspended is not considered one of the four primary triads, but I think it's important to discuss it, as the chord exists in many tunes and is quite useful. Suspended only has one "odd" note instead of two like diminished. This chord actually does fall within a key signature, usually major.

Key Signature

Even though there are four major chord qualities (five if you count suspended) there are only two possible key signature qualities, or keys. They are Major and Minor. There is no key signature to support augmented and diminished keys because they require accidentals. Therefore, they may be used as passing chords in a progression, but they do not have a key signature and cannot naturally exist as a tonic chord.

Except for the infrequent exceptions found in free jazz or fusion, you will likely never see a song where the fundamental tonality is augmented or diminished, only major or minor. It's like major and minor are natural particles, but augmented and diminished are man-made particles that do not exist outside a lab.

There are two kinds of Key Signature: Major and Minor. Augmented and Diminished do not exist as key signatures, only as chords.

Chord Extensions

Chord extensions add intervals to a chord for a more interesting or unique harmonic quality. Usually, the extensions to a chord are simply every other note, or an interval of a third up the associated scale, with only occasional exceptions.

The usual extensions are: 6th, 7th, 9th, 11th, and 13th. All extensions may be specified as flat, sharp, or natural.

Let's look at an easy example. The CMaj7 chord consists of C, E, G, B.

Below, a C Maj7 chord is depicted on the Grand Staff.

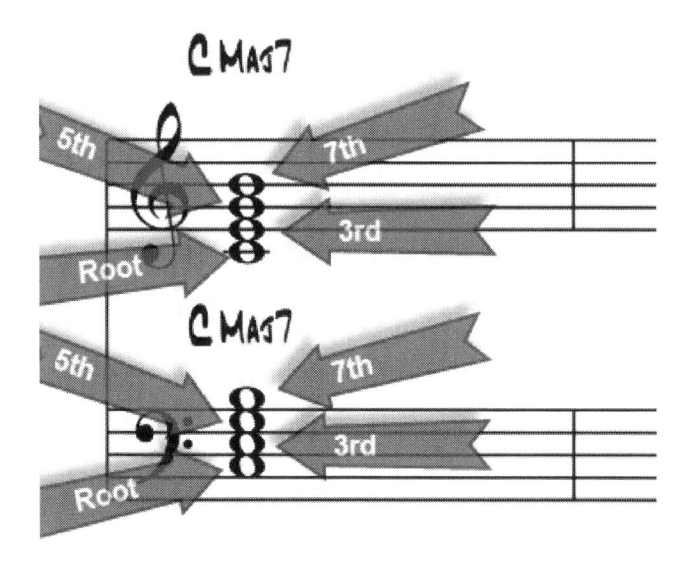

Notice that if you observe a C Major scale, the chord is made up of every other note in the scale, starting with the first note, or Keynote, which becomes the Root pitch of the chord.

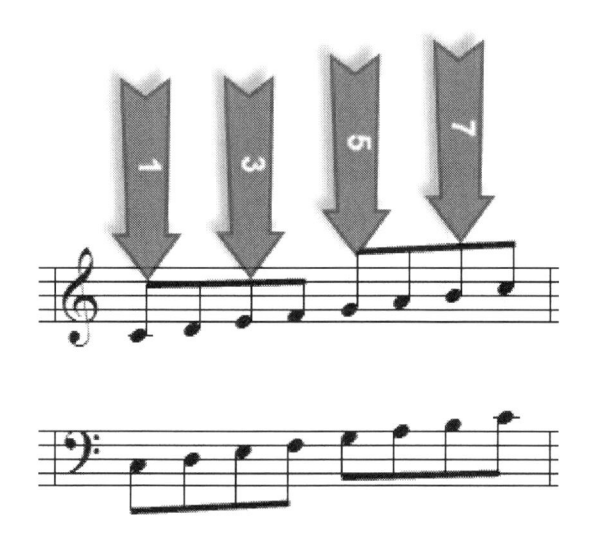

With this in mind, could you add another third? Sure you could! Accomplished improvisers do it all the time, without being asked or told. It's practically expected of you.

Using that CMaj7 (C, E, G, B)... you just continue playing up your Major scale to the next third above B. Let's recap - you have C, E, G, B. Now just go up another third (two notes on your associated scale). We have B, we pass C and come to D. There you have it – D is the next extension. You have added an extension to your CMaj7 chord, making it a CMaj 9 chord! Play this on a piano or play an arpeggio on your instrument: C, E, G, B, D…. That sounds very jazzy, no matter who plays it!

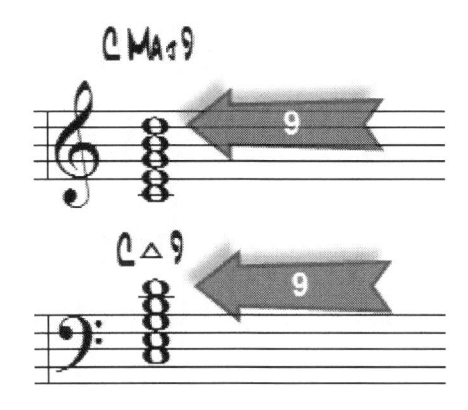

C Maj9

C △ 9

Don't stop there, let's continue. So you have your D. Let's go up another third. You should get F.

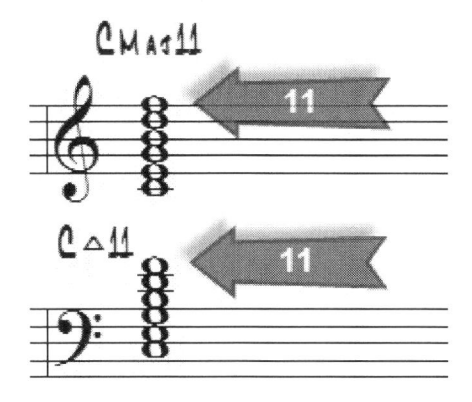

C Maj11

C △ 11

Jazz Improvisation FUNDAMENTALS

Things will start to get very dissonant now if you played this on piano because you are playing nearly every note in the scale all at one time. A good jazz piano player will know how to voice this so it sounds nice, but that is a topic for another time.

You should have noticed that all the extensions are *usually* every other note in the scale, starting with the root pitch. Of course, there is an exception to every rule, but I am a big fan of learning the standard musical rules so you understand what's going on before learning exceptions to the rule.

All chords are built from the scale's numeric pitch intervals. Therefore, you can build a chord within nearly any appropriately associated scale like so:

- The chord's root is the same as the first note (Keynote) of an associated scale.

- The chord's 3rd is derived from the third note in the scale.

- The chord's 5th is the fifth note in the scale.

- The 6th is the sixth note in the scale.

- The 7th is derived from the seventh note in the scale.

- The 9th is derived from the ninth (or second) note of the scale.

- The 11th is derived from the eleventh (or fourth) note in the scale.

- The 13th is derived from the thirteenth (or sixth) note in the scale.

You won't extend to the 15th because it would be the same note as the root, just two octaves up. There is no need to reiterate the root; it's already stated by the chord symbol. So if the chord in question is CMaj13, and someone asks you what the 15th is... it's C, just like the root.

Below, the circled note depicts redundant notes, showing why extensions to the 15th are unnecessary.

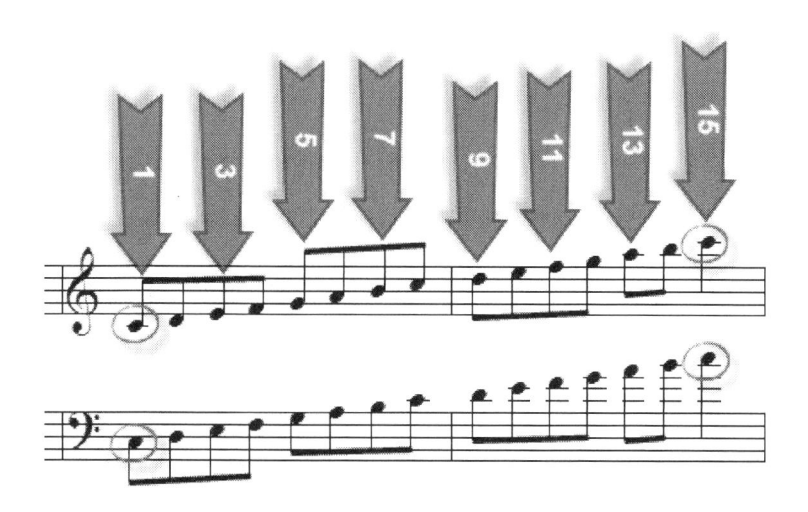

Chord Purpose

Chord tones are the basic outline of a song. They are harmonic structure, sort of like the frame of a house.

Sometimes you can identify a song by just hearing a chord progression even if the melody is not present because the chords provide you an audible outline. In fact, a song can be reduced to a few simple elements: tones from associated scales played over chords, usually set to a rhythm or beat.

Since chords provide the harmonic outline of a song, you can play any chord tone at any time and sound perfectly correct and resolved. Furthermore, you are not the only one playing chord tones – the entire rhythm section is plays them, too. They give you the harmonic outline with which to improvise your solo.

Eventually, you should strive to play more than simple chord tones. Nonetheless, they will make up a large portion of your solo, perhaps as much as 50% of your solo, but that is a very rough estimate.

As you advance, challenge yourself to perform a dissonant solo by "playing on the outside", purposely avoiding chord tones and preferring passing tones. All the same, chord tones are the walls of your solo, and you can always come back to them.

Chord Tones Are Safe Tones

I often refer to chord tones as Safe Tones, because you can *"never go wrong"* when playing them.

Below, an example of Chord Tones, or "Safe Tones".

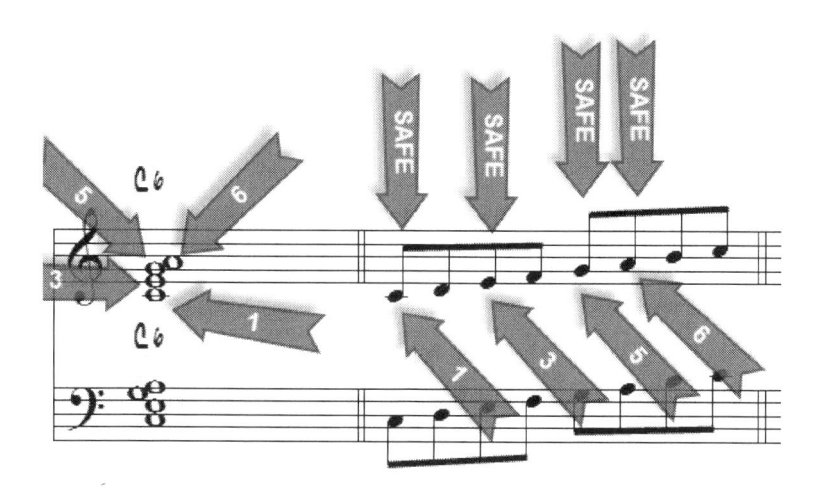

I am quite fond of pointing out that Coltrane's legendary *"Giant Steps"* solo starts with a basic ascending minor triad in root position, which associates perfectly with the minor seventh chord he addresses. He actually plays all four tones of the minor seventh chord, but for simplicity I like to point out that 'Trane teaches us with his solo that playing a basic triad in root position is not beneath him, and quite important to jazz improvisers, especially considering he used them in his opening statement. Coltrane knew his triads, and you should too!

If you want to study triads in depth, check out my book, <u>Jazz Triads</u>. It will give you a serious triad workout!

Step-1 Summary

- You must be able to decipher a chord, and all its chord tones.

- A triad is a three-note chord, with a Root, 3rd, and 5th.

- Chords are built from degrees of an associated scale.

- Chord tones could be altered (raised or lowered) to create Augmented or Diminished chords.

- All chords have a basic triad plus extensions.

- Common chord extensions are: 6th, 7th, 9th, 11th, and 13th.

- Chord extensions could be flat, natural or sharp.

- Chord Tones (Safe Tones) are the most appropriate notes you can play.

Step 2

Associate a Scale

Step-2 Associate a Scale

If you already know how to associate an appropriate scale to a chord (Chord/Scale) then you may skip ahead to Step-3, that's the fun part where you pick up your instrument and play. If not, then please read on.

After you have deciphered the chord, you will then associate an appropriate scale. As stated earlier, the scale you associate to the chord should contain scale pitches that match the chord tones. The scale you select should contain the chord's Root, 3rd, 5th, 7th, etc. Because the scale is so closely associated with the chord, we refer to this as a Chord Scale, or Chord/Scale. It is literally the chord's matching or associated scale, and vice-versa.

To do this, you will need to consult a Chord Scale Association Syllabus. We have one at our website for free. Just go here and download it: www.OgormanMusic.com/free-stuff

Here is an example of what I mean. Consider the chord in question is a CMaj7.

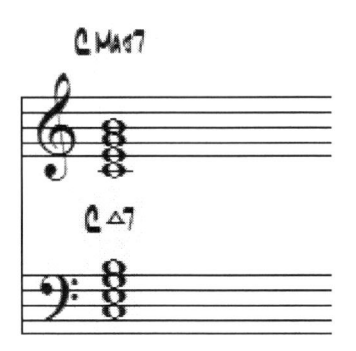

(musical notation: CMaj7 chord in treble and bass clef)

If you consult a chord scale syllabus, you should find the C Major scale, or Ionian scale, is perfect. You could also try the C Lydian, but perhaps we should use that later. Let's select the C Major scale.

Below, part of a Chord Scale Association Syllabus.

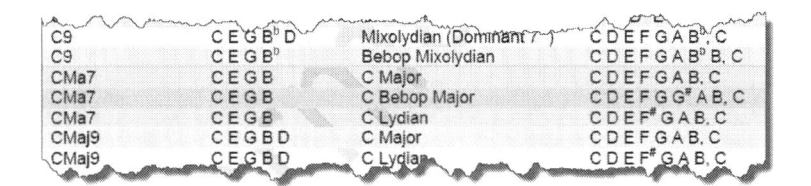

C9	C E G B♭ D	Mixolydian (Dominant 7)	C D E F G A B♭ C
C9	C E G B♭	Bebop Mixolydian	C D E F G A B♭ B C
CMa7	C E G B	C Major	C D E F G A B C
CMa7	C E G B	C Bebop Major	C D E F G G# A B C
CMa7	C E G B	C Lydian	C D E F# G A B C
CMaj9	C E G B D	C Major	C D E F G A B C
CMaj9	C E G B D	C Lydian	C D E F# G A B C

The chord is C Maj 7 = C, E, G, B. It looks like a C Major scale is an appropriate choice. The scale tones in the C Major scale are: C, D, E, F, G, A, B, C.

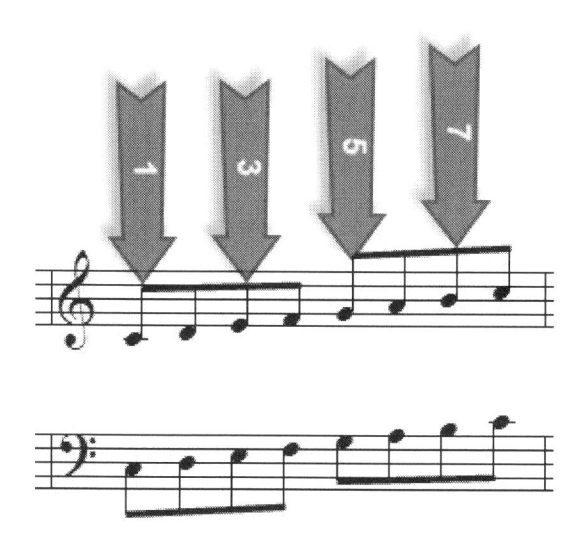

Notice in the C Major scale above the:

- First note (or Keynote) is the same as the chord's Root, which is C.

- Third note matches the chord's 3rd: E.

- Fifth note matches the chord's 5th: G.

- Seventh note matches the chord's 7th: B.

Jazz Improvisation Fundamentals

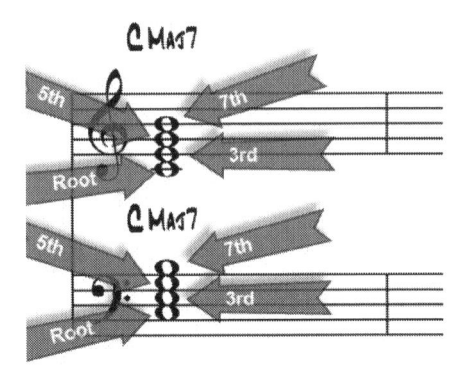

Perhaps now you clearly see why chords like this have four notes, but are called Root, 3rd, 5th, and 7th, rather than the first, second, third and fourth note.

An Associated Scale's KEYNOTE should match the Chord's ROOT.

Tones in a Chord Scale

Every scale has a defined set of tones or pitches. We call these Scale Tones. Only the notes (or pitches) in the scale are considered scale tones. All the chromatics in between are called chromatic passing tones. You are free to use chromatic passing tones when you improvise, but they are not classified as scale tones.

During improvisation (or even composing a symphony) Scale Tones are your most logical choices. If you selected the appropriate scale to associate with a chord, then all the tones in the scale (Scale Tones) will sound correct when played along with (or against) the chord.

We can break the scale tones down into two categories: Chord Tones and Passing Tones.

Chord Tones

Chord Tones (CT) always sound true and correct when played. If you are ever at a loss to play something, choose a chord tone! The most obvious chord tone is the Root, but you should be equally proficient playing the 3rd, 5th, or 7th. There are a few exceptions to this, but that advanced concept is for later study.

Below, a chord scale with the Chord Tones depicted.

Passing Tones

There are two kinds of Passing Tones (PT): Scale Passing Tones and Chromatic Passing Tones.

Below, a chord scale with the Passing Tones depicted.

Scale Passing Tone

This is any scale tone that is not already classified as a chord tone. In other words, every other note in your particular scale.

Below, re-using the previous image to show a chord scale with the <u>SCALE</u> Passing Tones depicted, i.e, only tones that are naturally included in the scale without chromatics.

Chromatic Passing Tone

As previously stated, all the chromatics in between the scale tones are called Chromatic Passing Tones. You are free to use chromatic passing tones when you improvise, in fact they will bring your solo to life. Without them your solo will be rather mechanical sounding.

I prefer you get very proficient with Chord Tones and Scale Passing Tones before adding Chromatics so that you demonstrate complete understanding and ability with the basics. However when you are ready, feel free to spice things up with chromatic passing tones.

Below, a chord scale with the <u>CHROMATIC</u> Passing Tones circled.

Step-2 Summary

- Scales are associated to Chords and vice-versa.

- Appropriate Scales contain the Chord Tones of your chord.

- The notes in a scale are called Scale Tones.

- Scale Tones can be Chord Tones or Passing Tones.

- Passing Tones may be Scale Tones, or Chromatic Tones.

- Scales are like a painter's palette, they color your solos. Different scales offer a different set of colors (tones) to work with.

Step 3

Play a Tone

Step-3 Play a Tone

Before you proceed, you must understand chords and how to associate a scale. If you don't understand that, then go back and read step one or two, because this section is where the rubber hits the road!

Now that you have matched a scale to a chord, what do you do with it, play the scale? No, that would be corny. You use pieces and parts of the scale. This is called Tone Selection. You apply a cool motif (melodic pattern of notes) to the scale and play those tones! How do you do that?

All you have to do now is select and play either a Chord Tone, or a Passing Tone. That's it. Really – That's it!

Anything else you are ever taught about jazz improvisation, any solo you ever transcribe, any song you ever play – no matter how difficult – can be reduced to a series of Chord Tones (CT) and Passing Tones (PT). That's why I strongly wish to teach you to use CT and PT as the building blocks of your solo. You can create anything with them. Even if someone is playing extensions and substitutions, it's all CT/PT.

We are about to practice one chord to make things easy. However, when you are playing a complete song, you will apply this concept to every chord in your music. Since that may prove too much for a new improviser, we'll begin with just one chord.

Another way I like to express this whole process:

1. Chord Identification

2. Scale Association

3. Tone Selection*

* Tone Selection, meaning "Select a tone and play it."

Here we go – Time to play!

I prefer you do this exercise by yourself, no other instruments. I want you to hear yourself as you play these things. Discover and begin to make decisions on what sounds good to you personally.

However, I know it's always more fun for you if you have a live band or a play-along to practice with.

We have a play-long online just for this purpose, called "JIF Practice". Find it at www.OGormanMusic.com/Videos

Get your Chord Scale Association Syllabus

If you need one, get one from our website under Free Stuff. www.OGormanMusic.com/Free-Stuff

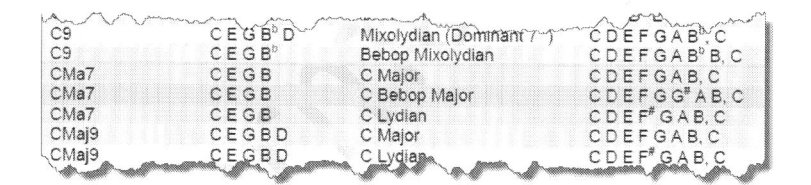

C9	C E G B♭ D	Mixolydian (Dominant 7)	C D E F G A B♭ C
C9	C E G B♭	Bebop Mixolydian	C D E F G A B♭ B, C
CMa7	C E G B	C Major	C D E F G A B, C
CMa7	C E G B	C Bebop Major	C D E F G G# A B, C
CMa7	C E G B	C Lydian	C D E F# G A B, C
CMaj9	C E G B D	C Major	C D E F G A B, C
CMaj9	C E G B D	C Lydian	C D E F# G A B, C

Step-1 Recap

Our Chord is C Maj7. By now you should remember the chord tones are C, E, G, B.

Step-2 Recap

Use the Chord Scale Syllabus to find a scale that goes with CMaj7. You should discover several, but the C Major Scale is the most obvious and appropriate choice.

There you go! You have associated a scale to the chord. To say that another way, you have made a chord/scale association. Now you are going to play it.

Take up your instrument. Stick with quarter notes or eighth notes at a very slow tempo for now.

Play the CMaj7 chord: C, E, G, B.

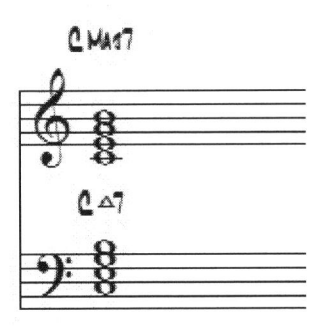

Then play your C Major scale one or two times, both ascending and descending (up and down).

Improvise

Rhythms

I suggest quarter-notes or eighth-notes to the beginner. Rhythm choice is a topic for another time. Right now, being able to select tones is the most important thing. Besides, if you have done any homework on your transcriptions, you see that most of the great jazz musicians play *mostly* eighth-note runs during a solo, with a few triplets and other syncopated ideas thrown in. You must be able to master a short eighth-note run before anything else.

Now using only the tones from your C Major scale (don't use any chromatics outside the scale yet):

1. Pick any Chord Tone (C) and play it.

2. Then any Passing Tone (P).

3. Repeat #1 and #2.

Below, Chord Tones are circled in blue, passing tones in yellow.

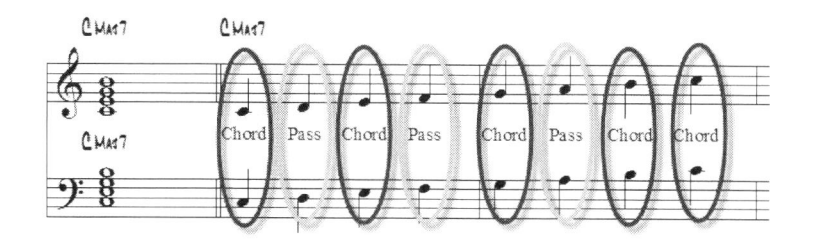

Now, stop here and practice that a few times before you read further.

Remember that you don't have to always go up the scale. You can go down the scale too, at will. Jump around as you wish, picking out chord tones and passing tones.

When you are ready, read on....

Now let's pick any chord tone (C), then any passing tone (P), then two more chord tones. Like this: CPCC. Stop and practice that against your C Major scale. After you try it a few times, read on.

This pattern (and patterns like it) will always sound perfect when used properly.

This is just one of a million patterns you could play. You can put CT or PT anywhere you wish.

For starters, I will pick some for you to play. Play them in the order listed.

PLAY...

4-Note Pattern:

- Chord Tone = B
- Passing Tone = A
- Chord Tone = G
- Chord Tone = E

6-Note Pattern:

- Passing Tone = F
- Passing Tone = A
- Chord Tone = G
- Passing Tone = F
- Chord Tone = E
- Chord Tone = G

...or any length pattern that sounds good or feels good to you!

Below, the 4 and 6 note patterns shown on the Grand Staff.

- *The first four notes are the four-note pattern previously discussed.*

- *The six notes following that are the six-note pattern previously discussed.*

This short example shows how several patterns can be strung together to create one whole riff or statement.

Can you make more like this? Give it a try right now!

Improv Exercise

Still using the C Major scale over a C Major chord, and sticking with quarter-notes or eighth-notes, try this:

- Try to make an easy four-note pattern, and play it.

- Make and play several four-note patterns.

- Play all your patterns together for a longer statement.

- Try exiting your new solo with a 5-note pattern.

From here on out, let's call Chord Tones "C" and Passing Tones "P", with respect to creating motifs or melodic patterns. This way we can represent nice-sounding patterns like CPCC, or CCPC. If you are actually performing this now, it should sound good to you, even without a band or backing track.

If this is all new to you, pick notes that are close to each other so you do not have to perform wild octave jumps or anything overly difficult. Keep it simple.

Okay, you should be improving, so try it!

Perform a CCPC on the CMAJ7 using the appropriately associated C Major Scale:

1. Play any chord tone.

2. Then play any passing tone.

3. Then play any chord tone.

4. Then another chord tone.

- Practice the short riff you created several times until you can play it with ease.

- Then make a new riff using the CCPC pattern, but pick different notes.

- Now play those two riffs back to back. You should have a nice run forming.

Change It Up

Instead of CPCC, try:

- CCPC
- PPCC
- CCPP

Try any combination of chord-tone/passing-tone you can think of. String these riffs together and you will soon have a solo that sounds like many of your favorite jazz heroes.

Once you get comfortable, add the chromatic notes that do not exist naturally within your chosen chord scale. Your chromatics will be used as passing tones, and can be used within the CP method just like any scale passing tone.

It really gets fun when you start to use extensions and substitutions, but I don't recommend you try those until you master these basics.

If you can master the CP method, you will always be able to build your own solos without help, transcripts, and pattern books. Later, when you begin to explore extensions and substitutions, you can still use the CP method on those advanced levels of improvisation.

Step-3 Summary

- Observe your Chord Scale.

- Identify the Chord Tones and Passing Tones.

- Play a Chord Tone, then a Passing Tone.

- Try to make easy four-note patterns using CPCC.

- String them all together for a longer statement.

- Try exiting your solo with a 5-note statement, ending strongly on a downbeat with a Chord Tone, such as: CPCPC.

- Repeat that process building longer and longer motifs, statements, riffs, runs, licks, or patterns (whatever you prefer calling them).

Improvisation Challenges

Improv Challenges

After you get the hang of the CP method, try this to challenge yourself:

Consonant Chord Tone Challenge

Use only chord tones to improvise. No passing tones, just chord tones. Play them any way you wish, any inversion, any octave.

Below, an example solo using only chord tones.

Can you create something similar?

Dissonant Passing Tone Challenge

Try to play dissonant. Use only passing tones, few or no chord tones. Play the Passing Tones as long as you can before resolving back into chord tones.

Below, example starting out using only passing tones before modulating back to chord tones for resolution.

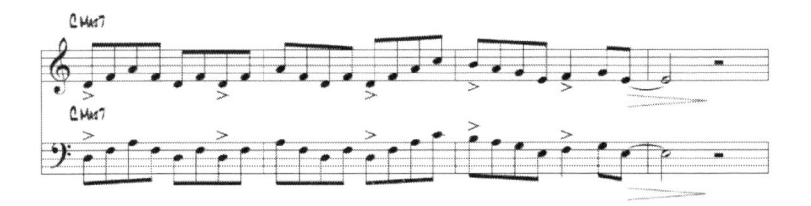

Can you create something similar?

Chromatic Chord Tone Challenge

Try to play only chord tones, however before each chord tone, play a chromatic pick-up or grace note. This will help you learn to use non-chord tones on the down beat, an advancing idea for a new improviser.

Below, an example of chord tones with grace-notes and chromatic down-beat (a kind of pick-up) preceding the chord tones which are on the up-beats.

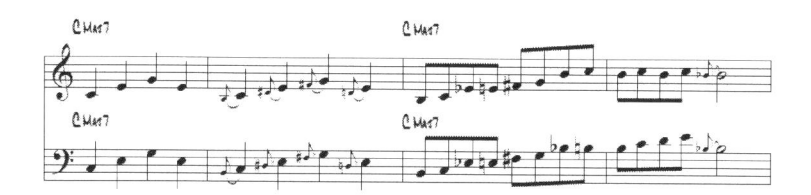

Can you create something similar?

Chromatic Passing Tone Challenge

Play only passing tones, but put a chromatic pick-up or grace note before each passing tone.

Below, an example of passing tones with chromatic grace-notes, resolving back to chord tones.

Can you create something similar?

Creative Freedom Challenge

Now take everything you have learned and play freely. No constraints. Use any combination of Chord Tones and Passing Tones with chromatics.

For a Play-Along with full jazz combo rhythm section, go here:

http://ogormanmusic.com/videos/

…and find the JIF Play-Along. It looks like this:

Videos
Check out videos of our products to see and hear how cool they are!

JIF Play-Along
for Jazz Improvisation Fundamentals

For more help and explanantions for this play-along, please check out the book:

Jazz Improvisation Fundamentals

www.OGormanMusic.com

Jazz Improvisation Fundamentals

Start the Play-Along and use the slashed Sheet Music below. It won't change from CMaj7; the purpose is to practice your fundamentals.

Below is the sheet music with slash notation, which is where you improvise.

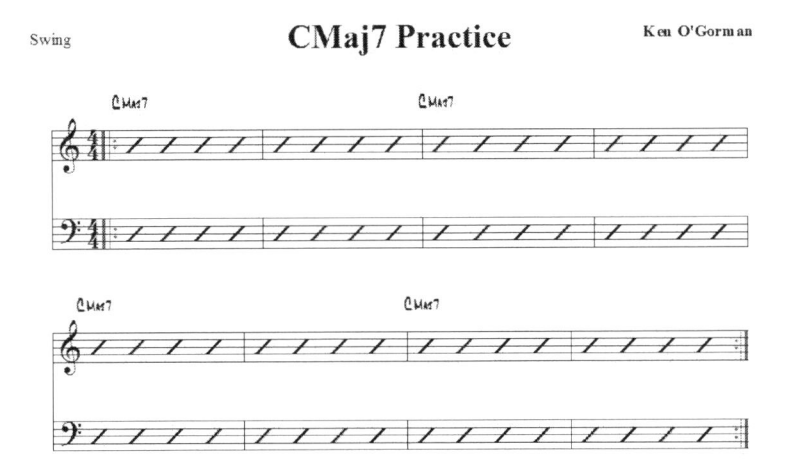

Remember to use tones from the C Major scale to create your solos.

Below, the C Major Chord and C Major Scale already associated for you.

Exceptions to the Rule

You will soon run into a few exceptions. I dislike talking about exceptions or advanced concepts with beginners. It's like putting the cart before the horse. However, you will encounter these exceptions very shortly. You may even be challenged by a lesser player, or worse – a lesser jazz instructor who should know better. Here are a few exceptions you should know right away:

Below, an example of exceptions to the rule. Blues scale associated to the C Dominant 7 scale.

Many jazz instructors teach this as the FIRST scale to use on C7. I highly disagree. The most appropriate scale to associate with any Dominant 7th chord is a Dominant 7th scale, i.e., a Mixolydian scale. This kind of direct association allows you to hear how the scale's Keynote, 3rd, 5th and 7th, etc., sound against the chord's Root, 3rd, 5th and 7th. They match perfectly and sound good.

The Blues scale is actually an exception to the rule. It has several points of confusion for the novice. However, I do encourage its use, but only after you understand how the common associations work. The Blues scale *theoretically* looks like it shouldn't work, at least on paper.

Allow me to expand on why the Blues scale is an exception to the rule, and should not be taught as a *primary* chord scale association to the novice.

- The Blue scale has no 2nd. The second note of the scale is actually considered a 3rd, a potential point of confusion for the novice.

- The second note of the Blues scale is the note that corresponds to the third in the Dom7 chord. This loss of chord/scale numeric alignment leads to a point of confusion for the novice.

- Using the Blues scale's second note as the third leads to a chromatic clash (which actually sounds good but looks theoretically wrong). This is a point of confusion to the novice.

- The third note of the blues scale is actually the 4th against the Chord's 3rd which leads to a point of confusion for the novice.

- The third note of the Blues scale, the 4th as described above, falls on the down beat. Usually in jazz, the novice will find that chord tones (rather than passing tones) falling on the down beat sounds more resolved.

- The blues scale's 5th note is a half-step lower than the 5th in the chord. This dissonance leads to a point of confusion for the novice learning basic harmony.

- The 5th note in the blues scale injects a second 4th. This scale harmonically has two 4ths, leading to a potential point of confusion for the novice.

- The blues scale is a 6-note scale. When played, it has an unbalanced feel unless against a common 4/4 time signature which leads to a point of difficulty for the novice.

Below, a better way to practice the Blues scale so that it feels good in 4/4 time (this is only one possible variation).

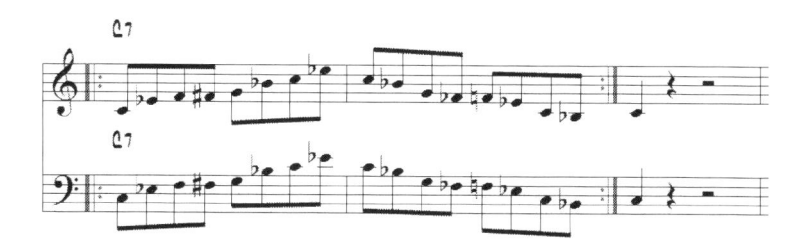

For the record, I do not hate the Blues scale and I am not down on you using it. I use it myself. But before you go there, you should understand basic harmony choices, like the sound of a scale's Major 3rd against the chord's Major 3rd, or Minor 7th, etc. Get that down first, then you can begin to advance into harmonic exceptions. Starting with the Blues scale first just creates confusion in an already confusing subject.

Other Scale Choices

There are other scales than the ones I am showing you. In fact, there are a ton of scales you can associate with chords. I won't overload you with every possible scale, let's stick with common choices. If you cannot improvise using easy common chord scale associations, then advanced scales or substitutions will just leave your head spinning.

Once you grasp the basics of improv, moving on to difficult and less obvious chord scale combinations will make much more sense.

Below, notice several scale possibilities for CMaj7, highlighted in yellow.

C9	C E G B♭ D	Mixolydian (Dominant 7)	C D E F G A B♭ C
C9	C E G B♭	Bebop Mixolydian	C D E F G A B♭ B, C
CMa7	C E G B	C Major	C D E F G A B, C
CMa7	C E G B	C Bebop Major	C D E F G G# A B, C
CMa7	C E G B	C Lydian	C D E F# G A B, C
CMaj9	C E G B D	C Major	C D E F G A B, C
CMaj9	C E G B D	C Lydian	C D E F# G A B, C

Minor Over Major

You can play minor over major. Let's use C7 as an example. The C7 chord is actually classed as a Dominant 7th chord and provides a "Dominant" sound. Let's examine the basic triad. Notice it's a plain old major triad. It's basic quality sounds Major, as opposed to minor, diminished, or augmented. Therefore, you would normally associate and perform scales that includes a Major 3rd, (and minor 7th) rather than a scale with a minor 3rd.

However, you can usually play a Blues scale over a dominant 7th. That is, play a C Blues scale over the C7 chord.

But wait – the C7 has a *major* 3rd and the Blues scale has a *minor* 3rd. Will that sound horrible? No. In fact, it sounds great. Many jazz and blues greats use blues scales exclusively over dominant 7th chords in particular scenarios.

Consider the Blues scale on the next page. It is often used over a Dominant 7th chord. Notice the minor 3rd in the C Blues scale creates a chromatic clash against the Major 3rd in the C Dom7 chord.

In jazz, this is perfectly okay, and an example of an exception to the rules of harmony: Minor over Major.

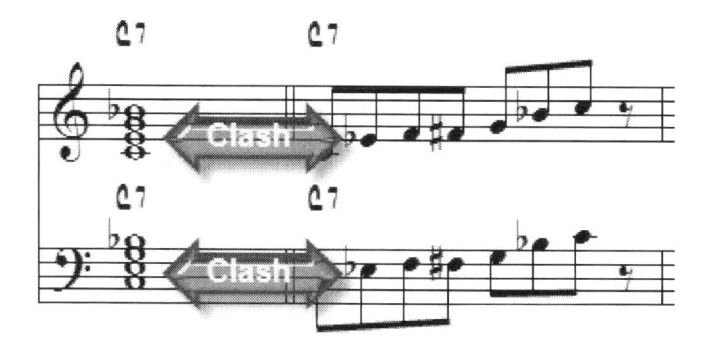

Personally, I would use the C Mixolydian or C Bebop Mixolydian, or a few other advanced scale choices, but a C Blues scale will sound rather cool, and everybody does it. So there is your Minor over Major example.

Below, the C Bebop Mixolydian scale perfectly associates to the C Dominant 7th Chord.

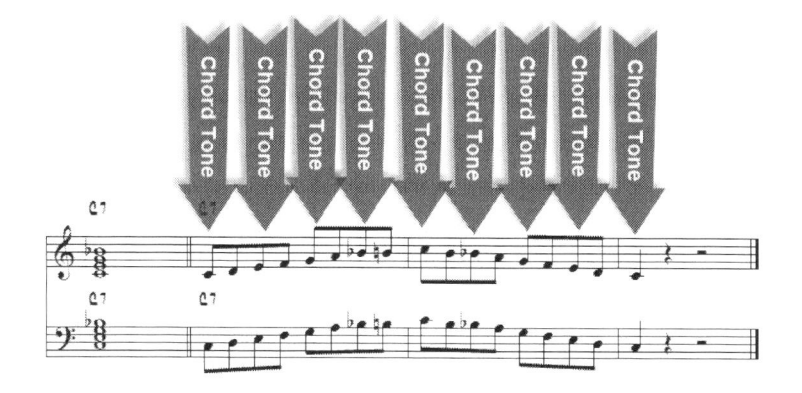

Avoid the Root

Many famous jazz musicians give this improvisation tip: Avoid the Root. That is so you don't sound boring. Think about it, the bass player is playing the root quite frequently. S/he is doing so using one of their many techniques, such as "biads" (a root/5th technique) or "walking" the scale. The piano player is playing the whole chord and has the root covered in most cases. The guitar and vibes maybe be playing the root as well, although if they are skilled, they will play extensions to ensure different parts of the chord are covered.

So, you see, there are a lot of people playing the root. Now it's your turn to solo. What shall you do... play the root, too? *BORING!* You are a jazz musician; do something more interesting!

Try starting your solo on the 3rd, the 5th, or the 7th. Add a 9th or a passing tone if you want to, but for goodness sake, avoid the root... everyone else just played it!

Also in a few cases, like with Flat 9 chords, or Major 7 Sharp 11 chords, the rhythm section may elect to drop the root to favor the extensions that are more interesting than the root. In short, the "Avoid the Root" tip encourages you to explore other chord tones, and upper extensions.

That being said, please remember – it's an exception to the rule, geared towards advancing jazz improvisers. If you are just learning, or otherwise struggling with jazz improvisation concepts, then ignore this exception until you get better. Go ahead and play the root. I want you to. Prove to me you understand the tones in the chords you encounter by playing the root, the 3rd, the 5th, or an extension of the current chord. You have my express permission!

Below, an easy solo using only tones from the associated chord scale, while avoiding the performance of the Root in each chord.

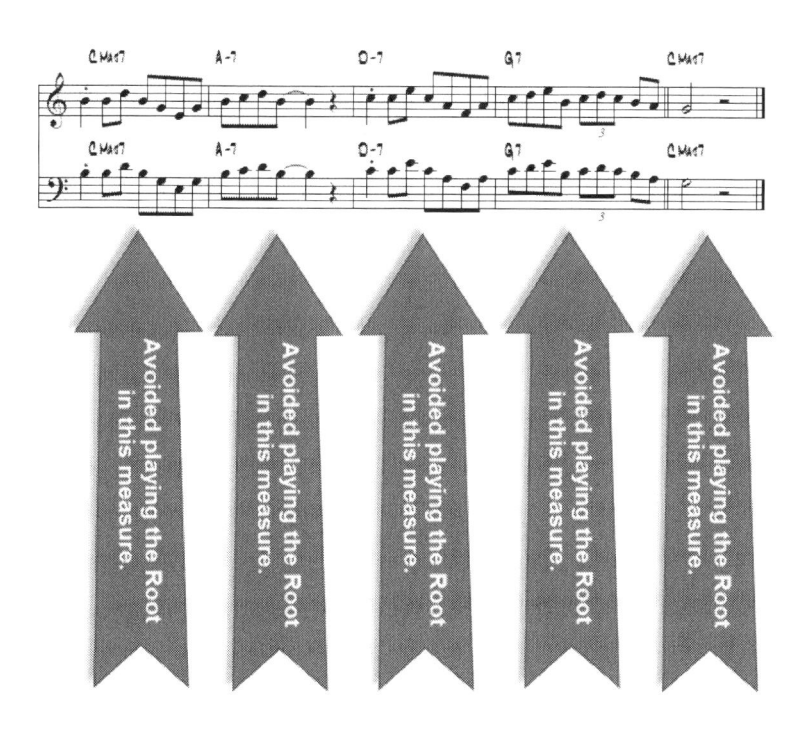

When the 3rd is NOT the 3rd

Usually the third note of a scale is the same as the chord's 3rd. There are a few exceptions to that rule which jazz musicians must know.

Here is one example: C7(b9), which spoken aloud is "C Seven Flat-Nine". The chord tones are: C, E, G, Bb, Db.

This is a typical "Flat-Nine" (or b9) chord. A jazz musician's favorite scale to associate with it is the Half-Whole Diminished. It's a gorgeous sounding scale I highly encourage you to learn as soon as possible. The H-W Diminished scale has more tones than your average diatonic scale. It looks like this: C, Db, Eb, E, F#, G, A, Bb, C.

The scale tones satisfy the chord tones specified by the chord symbol. Conversely, the chord tones specified by the chord symbol are contained by the C H-W Diminished scale. Perfect!

Okay, let's start matching the root, third etc. in this example. Just to recap, we are addressing:

- **Chord:** C7(b9)
- **Associated Scale:** C Half-Whole Diminished
- **Chord Tones:** C, E, G, Bb, Db.
- **Scale Tones:** C, Db, Eb, E, F#, G, A, Bb, C

The first thing to notice is the Root matches the Keynote, the first note in a scale. We expected that, of course.

The second thing to notice is the 3rd of the chord is E, but the third note in the scale is Eb. Whoa – That's going to be dissonant! How's that going to work?

This is one of those exceptions you need to be aware of. In this particular example, the Eb is only a passing tone for you to use in your solo. The FOURTH note, the E natural, is the third of the chord, so that's the note you wish to use as the 3rd. Some people like to say this chord has two 3rds, an Eb and an E Natural with the E Natural being the most obvious choice if you wish to sound resolved.

Below, the C7(b9) chord associated with the C Half-Whole Diminished Scale, an example of when the 3rd is not the 3rd.

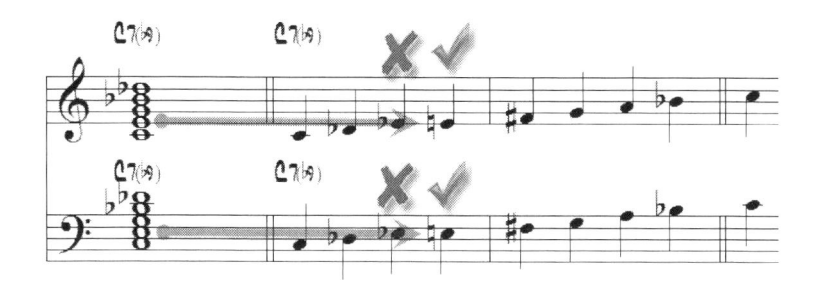

Jazz Improvisation Fundamentals

     As an improvising musician, you will always desire the chord tones match up with your scale tones, even if they wind up not being in the pitch sequence you would expect, as we just experienced with the association of the 3rd of a C7(b9) and the 4th note of the C Half-Whole Diminished scale.

     The third thing to notice is the 5th, which is "G" in the C7(b9). Again, we encounter the same exception problem we had deciphering the 3rd. The 5th is G, but the fifth note of the scale is F#. You know that is not going to sound good at all. Let's use our heads... what note do you suppose we should really use to address the 5th in the C7(b9) chord? If you answered "G", you are correct.

     Even though G is the sixth note in the C Half-Whole Diminished scale, it perfectly matches the 5th in the C7(b9) chord. Again, we are experiencing an exception to the rule, the chord's 5th matches the scale's 6th, in this particular example. But if we view this scale as having *two* 3rds in it (Eb and E Natural), then G really is the 5th note, and matches up without using an exception to explain why it works.

     The fourth thing to notice is something I hope you have already figured out. The 7th in the chord is Bb, which should match the seventh note in the scale, but that's "A". Bb is the match we want, but Bb is the eighth note (note number 8) in the scale, and usually the eighth note is the octave! What do you make of it? Again, we have two 3rds in this scale, so the Bb becomes the 7th note in the scale, matching the chord's

7th. Were you able to deduce that without explanation? If so you are well on your way to understanding the associations of chords and scales.

To complete this example, notice we have a b9 (flat-nine). Usually the 9 is the ninth note in the scale, and is the same note as the 2nd, but it's an octave higher. Keep in mind the scale we are using has two 3rds in it. That being the case, we can decipher the 9th is D, but the chord (and associated Half-Whole Diminished scale) *flats* the 9 (lowers the ninth from whatever it was in the scale by one-half step). If we lower/flat the D as directed by the scale construction for a H-W Dim scale, we get Db. The C H-W Dim scale, if you remember, consists of C, Db, Eb, E, F#, G, A, Bb, C. The b9 is easily covered by the lowered 2nd in the scale (Db), which if raised an octave, is the flat nine, Db.

Substitutions

If you are a beginner, you shouldn't attempt substitutions until you can improvise using the basic chords and scales already suggested by your music. However, you will eventually learn how to substitute the chords (and associated scale) with chords you'd rather play.

Most chords share a harmonic relationship with other chords, and therefore, in most cases, they can be swapped on the fly for a more interesting sound. Proficient rhythm sections are likely performing chord substitutions as you play and you didn't realize it. Some substitutions ("Subs") work because they are closely related to the original chord.

In the example below, I will show you how a chord within the chord can be thought of as an extension or a substitution. This is an easy common passing chord sequence used by chord players to modulate to a subdominant, but you could sit on this as a one-chord jam and experiment with the tonality as extension or a substitute chord to gain proficiency with the concept.

Consider this chord: C7. We casually call it a *C Seven*, or more formally, *C Dominant Seven or Seventh*. The Chord Tones are (C, E, G, Bb). With our C7, you would associate the appropriate scale. An obvious choice is C Mixolydian, (C, D, E, F, G, A, Bb, C).

Many jazz players would add a 9th for a really cool sound. In fact the 9th is often credited as "The Jazz Sound" because few genres outside jazz use the 9th or higher frequently. If you count the notes in your C Mixolydian, you find the 9th for a C7 is "D". The full chord just became C9 (C, E, G, Bb, D). Congratulations, you just performed your first chord extension! But that's still not quite a substitution, it's only an extension.

Below, adding an extension to a C7 to create a C9.

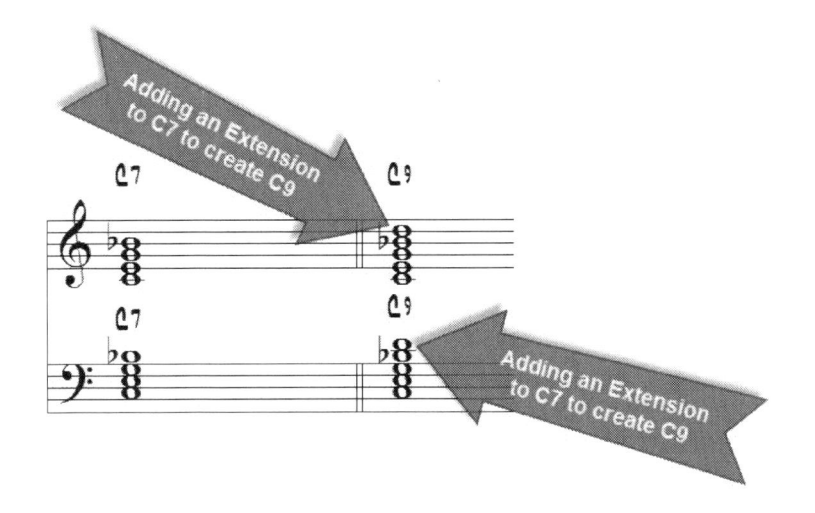

Now take a close look at what's hiding amidst our C9... a Gm triad! Start with the C9's 5th, which is G. Do you see the G, Bb, D? That is a G minor triad.

A Gm chord is hiding within your C7 chord, shown below.

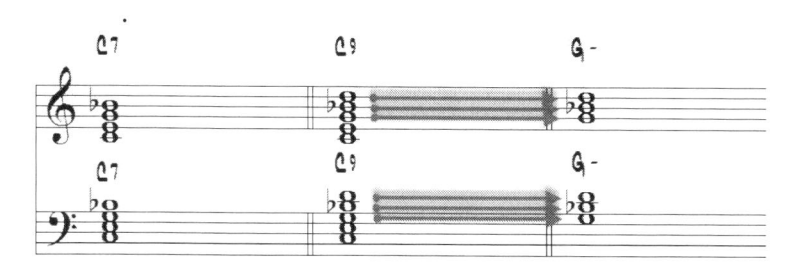

We already know that jazz and blues players like chord extensions. Most jazz or blues music has at least a 7th. Can we add a minor 7th to our new Gm substitution? Of course!

Your Gm substitution contains G, Bb, D. We have initially selected C Mixolydian or "C Mix" as our chord scale. We can continue to use this for the moment. In fact, let's go up another third from D, using our "C Mix". You should come to F. It's the 4th (or 11th, same thing) in a C7. However, "F" is also the 7th in the Gm... so by adding two extensions, you have created this Gm7 from your original C7.

Below, extending a G- to G-7.

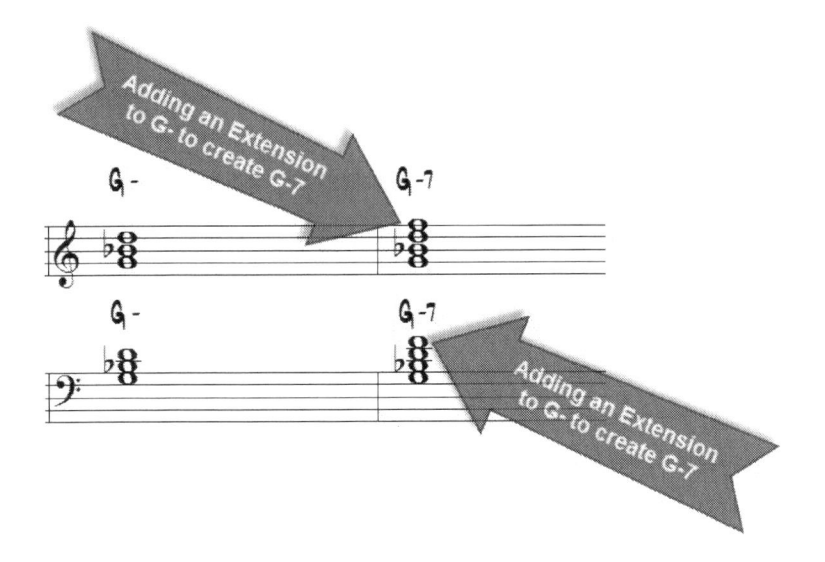

Now, even though the band is playing C7, you have replaced the chord with a Gm7. Therefore think Gm7 and solo on that using the G Dorian scale, which has an E natural as its 6th, which in turn jives perfectly with the "E" (the 3rd) in the C7.

Below, the G Dorian scale is associated with the C Dom7 Chord, rather than the usual C Mixolydian scale, so that you can emphasize the G-7 you created by extending the C7 chord.

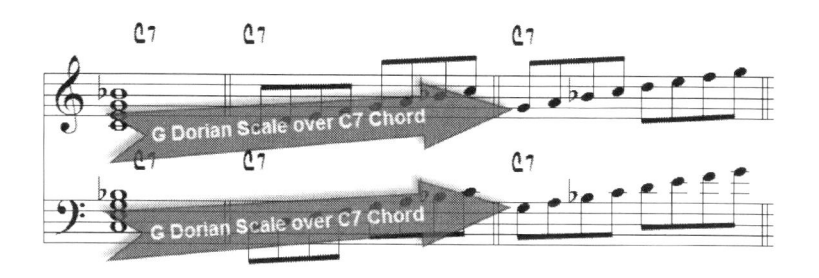

Now you can tell the world you are substituting Gm7 over C7, and using a G Dorian to solo, and it will sound great. All the newbies (noobs) will be asking you how you achieved that sound. Tell them all about your new chord substitute. And don't forget to tell them who taught you how. Who's your buddy?!?

In the above example, it may be wise to point out that if you sit on the F, in Gm7 too long it may sound unresolved. That's cool if you wanted that sound on purpose, but if you exit your statement or idea on something more resolved, like a chord tone from the original C7, your solo will sound like you know what you are doing.

Example: Resolve (play) the F to E, or F to G.

You just extended a chord, substituted the current chord (the one that everyone is actually playing) for one you'd rather play that is harmonically related, then resolved back to the current chord. Well played, musician. Well played!

Below:

Measure 1 – The original C7 chord

Measure 2 – Extending C7 to C9

Measure 3 – Finding the Gm triad with the C7

Measure 4 – Extending the Gm triad to Gm7

Remember Gm and G- mean the same thing.

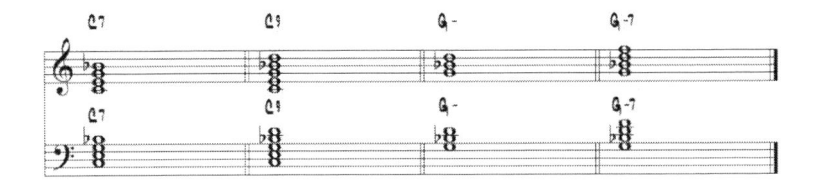

Staff Writing Exercise

The best improvisers don't just read, they write as well. It would be excellent practice and good experience to write a few ideas out on paper. Perhaps you can develop a few nice riffs to use at your next jam session. Or, see if someone else can read and play what you wrote. There is a certain satisfaction that comes from writing something and having someone else play it. Maybe you could even write a short "Head" or Song!

To help you get started, here is an easy staff writing exercise followed by staff paper.

- Pick an easy chord, write it above the staff, perhaps one of the four primary triads you learned earlier, or a Major 7th or Dominant 7th chord.

- Below the chord, write out the chord tones on the staff using whole notes.

- In the next measure write out a scale that associates with it. You can always use the Chord Scale Association Syllabus from our website, it's free. http://ogormanmusic.com/free-stuff/

- Pick out Chord Tones and Passing Tones from the scale at random and write them on the staff paper. I suggest using quarter notes and eighth notes.

- Now play the riff you wrote!

- Get someone else to play the riff you wrote.

- Then do it all again, but try a different chord.
- Then, try a different scale.

Remember if you wish to play your riffs with a rhythm section, but don't have a band, use our free online play-along located here (look for JIF play-along): http://ogormanmusic.com/videos/

Here are a few sheets of Treble Clef and Bass Clef staff paper so you can write down and develop any improv ideas that come to mind.

If you need more staff paper, get some free here: http://ogormanmusic.com/free-stuff/

Treble Staff Paper

Treble Staff Paper

Treble Staff Paper

Jazz Improvisation Fundamentals

Treble Staff Paper

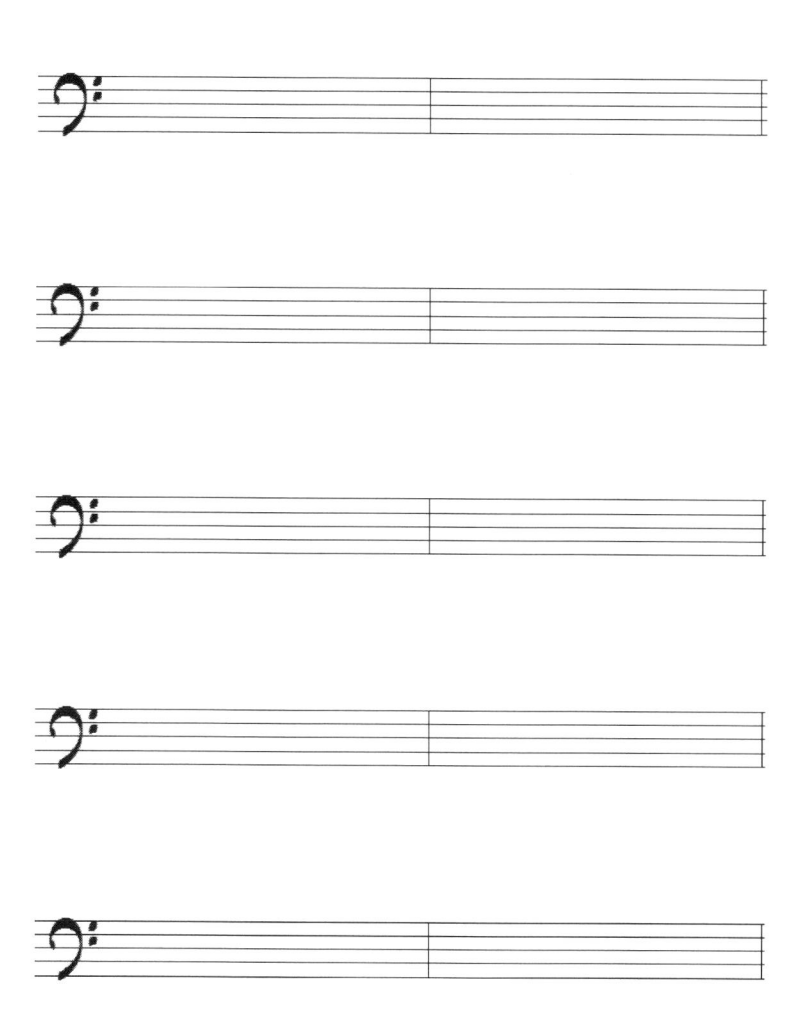

Jazz Improvisation Fundamentals

Bass Staff Paper

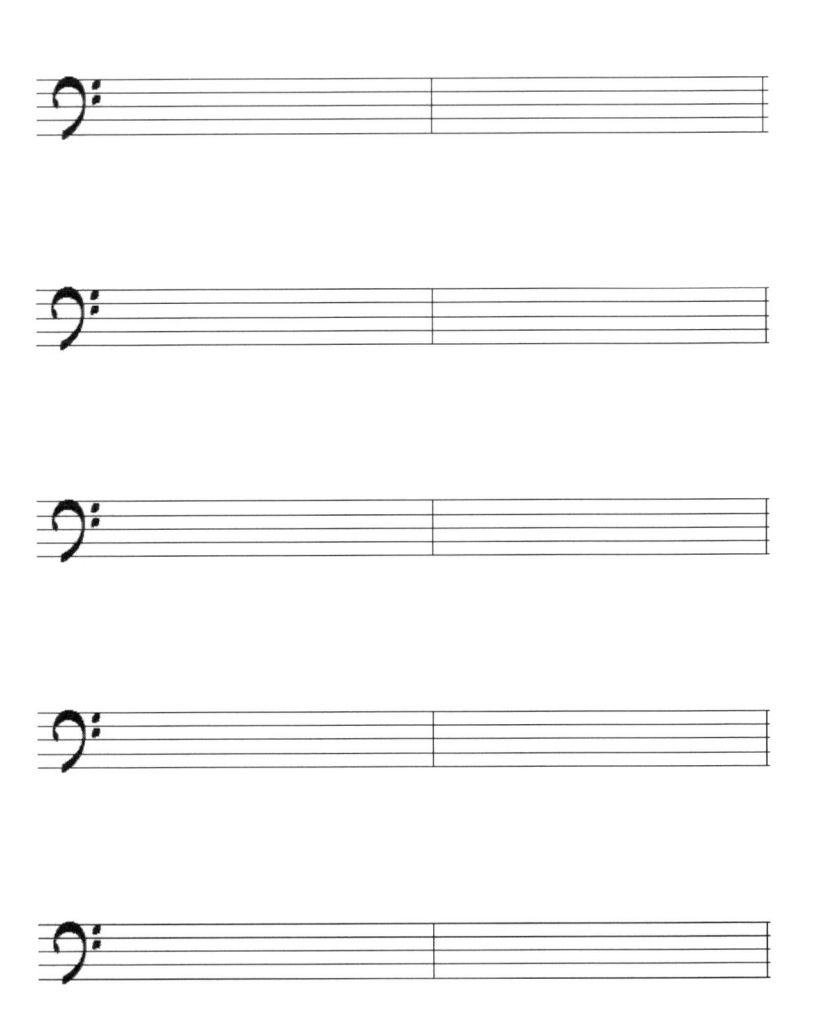

Jazz Improvisation Fundamentals

Bass Staff Paper

Bass Staff Paper

Jazz Improvisation Fundamentals

Bass Staff Paper

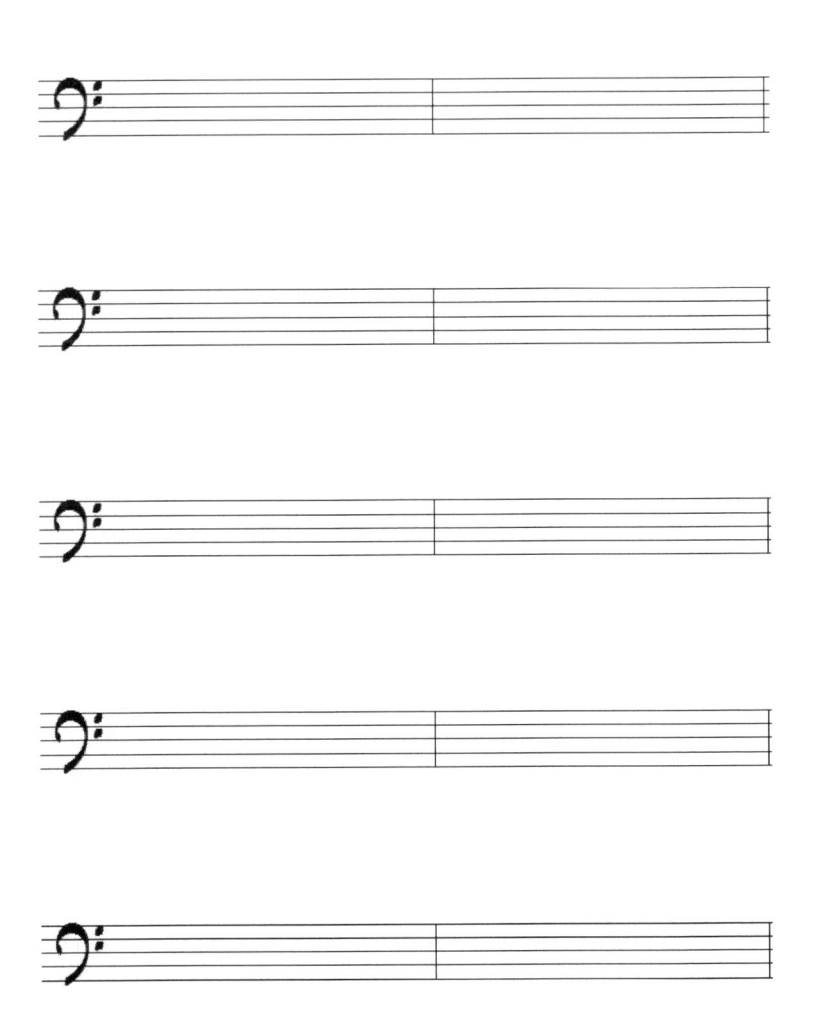

The End

This concludes Jazz Improvisation Fundamentals.

It was not so very long ago that I was a young struggling jazzer, learning the ropes and over-whelmed by all the possibilities. I can still relate to musicians who are new to jazz improvisation, or trying to advance their improvisation skills, and I do my very best to help you achieve your goals.

I truly hope the information in my book helped you gain new skills and valuable insight. Please check my website; I have several freebies available to help you, like the Chord and Scale Association Syllabus and the Modal Matrix, etc.

Be well, play well, and the best of gigs to you!

Sincerely,

Kenneth M. O'Gorman
OGormanMusic.com

Dear Reader,

Thank you for reading my book. I sincerely hope it gave you the encouragement and insight needed to study and practice jazz improvisation. I wrote this book because I wish there was a book like it when I was learning, full of graphics and images that help make a difficult subject like jazz much easier to comprehend.

If you feel this book helped you, would you please give it a review and a high star rating?

It truly helps authors know if people are reading our works or not, and provides encouragement to continue writing.

Thanks!
Ken

Index

Associate a Scale, 77
Augmented Triad, 57
Avoid the Root, 116
Biad, 11
Chart, 11
Chord, 12
Chord Construction, 13
Chord Extensions, 67
Chord Player, 12
Chord Progression (Progression), 14
Chord Scale, 15
Chord Scale Association Syllabus, 78
Chord Symbol, 37
Chord Tones, 15, 82
Chorus, 17
Chromatic Passing Tone, 85
Diminished Triad, 59
Dominant 7th Chord, 48
Enharmonic, 17
Exceptions to the Rule, 109
Extensions, 18, 47
Half-Diminished, 62
Head, 8, 18
Intro, 18
Jazz Improvisation, 5
Jazz Theory, 19
Last Four (Last 4), 19
Major Triad, 46
Melody, 19
Minor Over Major, 114
Minor Triad, 55
Minor-Seventh Flat-Five, 62
Monophonic Instrument, 20
Numeric Notation, 20
Outro, 21
Passing Chord, 22
Passing Tone, 22
Passing Tones, 83
Polyphonic Instrument, 23
Quality, 42
Rhythm Section, 24
Root, 40
Safe Tones, 73
Scale Passing Tone, 84
Slashed Notation, 24
Song Form AABA, 25
Staff Paper, 129
Substitutions, 26, 123
Terminology, 11
Tone Selection, 89
Tonic Chord, 28

Trade-Fours, 26
Triad, 30, 42
Tritone, 27
Turn-Around, 31

Undocumented Key
　Signatures, 51
Verse, 32
When the 3rd is NOT
　the 3rd, 118

Other Training Materials

by OGormanMusic.com

Music Books

- *Scales A La Mode*
  An Introduction to Modal Improvisation

- *Jazz Triads*
  Triad Arpeggios for Aspiring Jazz Musicians

- *Major and Minor Scales with Chords and Patterns*

- *Easy Classical for Beginners*
  Ten beloved classics by famous composers.

eBooks

- Jazz Improvisation Fundamentals (Abridged)

- Transpose Music

Play-Alongs

Download to your music player and practice today! Find us in any major online music store.

Jazz 2-5-1 Play-Along Practice Series
- Jazz 2-5-1 Practice Volume 01 (vi-ii-V-I)
- Jazz 2-5-1 Practice Volume 02 (VI-ii-V-I)
- Jazz 2-5-1 Practice Volume 03 (ii7b5-V7b5-i7-i7)

Blues Play-Along Practice Series
- Blues Practice, Volume 01 (Major/Shuffle)
- Blues Practice, Volume 02 (Minor/Shuffle)

Classical Play-Along
- Easy Classical for Beginners - Backing Tracks

Metronome Series
Because a plain old metronome is just boring!

- Jazz Metronome
- Bossa Nova Metronome
- Blues Shuffle Metronome
- Rock Metronome

Gift Items for Musicians
You can score some great musician swag at our gift shops. We have T-Shirts & Other Apparel, Mugs, Keychains, Jewelry, Phone Cases, Luggage Tags, Buttons & Stickers, Gift Wrap, etc.
- Search Amazon.com for O'Gorman Music
- Zazzle.com/OgormanMusic
- Cafepress.com/OgormanMusic

PLEASE DO NOT COPY THIS BOOK

The music business is tough enough, so I make this appeal to those who may be considering pirating honest work. Besides being illegal, copying a book hurts music education by discouraging authors and composers from publishing future material for you to study and enjoy.

The price for this book is quite reasonable when you consider the hundreds of hours , thousands of dollars, and decades of experience it takes to actually sit down to write, compose, edit, correct, copyright, publish, print and advertise a completed work for sale. It could take years just to break even from production costs. So if you find the information in this book convenient and valuable, please purchase a valid copy today!

Sincerely,
Kenneth M. O'Gorman

Made in the USA
Columbia, SC
26 December 2019